After
YOU'VE DRESSED
FOR
Success

Luci Swindoll

Other Books by Luci Swindoll

Wide My World, Narrow My Bed: Living and
Loving the Single Life

Wide My World, Narrow My Bed Study Guide

The Alchemy of the Heart: Life's Refining Process to
Free Us from Ourselves

You Bring the Confetti! The Celebration of Life

My Favorite Verse

A Guide to Developing

Character As Well As a Career

After
YOU'VE DRESSED
FOR
Success

Luci Swindoll

WORD BOOKS
PUBLISHER
WACO, TEXAS

A DIVISION OF
WORD, INCORPORATED

AFTER YOU'VE DRESSED FOR SUCCESS:
A GUIDE TO DEVELOPING CHARACTER AS WELL AS A CAREER

Scripture quotations in this book are from the following sources:

> *The Living Bible* (LB), copyright 1971 by Tyndale House Publishers, Wheaton, IL. Used by permission.
> The New American Standard Bible (NASB), © The Lockman Foundation 1960, 1962, 1963, 1968, 1971, 1972, 1973, 1975, 1977.

Thanks are extended to William Arthur Ward for permission to use his poem, "I Will Do More," as printed in a 1985 issue of *Successful Supervisor*.

Library of Congress Cataloging-in-Publication Data:

> Swindoll, Luci, 1932–
> After you've dressed for success.
>
> 1. Conduct of life. 2. Success. I. Title.
> BJ1581.2.S93 1988   248.8'8   88-5440
> ISBN 0-8499-0649-0

Printed in the United States of America

8 9 8 FG   9 8 7 6 5 4 3 2

Contents

Foreword

THE FACT IS, I've never really fit in.

Being a Christian working woman means that fellow Christians are skeptical at best of my ability to be committed to my faith as well as serious about my job. And when the fact comes out that I actually work because I love what I do, not because I *have* to, skepticism is sometimes replaced by open concern about my spiritual condition.

So I have learned to mumble when those at church ask me what I do; to downplay the fact that I use my talents in ways that I believe God has clearly ordained. I've given up explaining that my husband not only "puts up with" my work but encourages me and challenges me to be a growing, responsible professional.

But the reactions of those in the church are mild compared to what I sometimes encounter from my secular professional counterparts. Knowing I'm a Christian, they sometimes eye me suspiciously, wondering if I'm about to pounce on them with a condemnation of their lifestyle. One man announced, "I'll talk to you about publishing, but I don't want to hear anything about religion." Another friend confessed he sometimes worried that my professional judgment would be impaired by my "emotional religious interest."

And so, in many ways, I've learned to carve out my own idea of what it means to be a Christian woman in the working world. I love what I am and what I do, and if others misunderstand, it no longer bothers me.

But what fun it is to meet someone like Luci Swindoll, who not only practices what it means to be a Christian woman in a career, but who practices what she preaches in all that she does. When I first met Luci over coffee in a Washington, D.C., hotel, I immediately felt a kinship—at last, here was someone who understood me.

When I heard Luci was writing this book, I begged her to write it quickly, feeling like a desert traveler who has heard word that an oasis is just ahead. I needed this book, and I knew that there were other women like myself who would find it quenched their thirst for understanding.

After You've Dressed for Success is all that I hoped for and more. It is so refreshing, so encouraging, so hopeful about the role of the Christian working woman that I found myself walking a little taller after reading it. It made me feel grateful for this sometimes ambiguous role and challenged me to integrate my faith and my work to an even greater degree.

This book will change the life of every Christian working woman who reads it. And any woman still looking for her niche will find that she is several steps closer, thanks to Luci Swindoll's insights.

—DALE HANSON BOURKE
President, Publishing Directions
Senior Editor, *Today's Christian Woman*

Prologue

The
Journey

FOR FORTY-TWO YEARS I've been writing this book. That's a long time to spend on any one project, but it's the truth.

From my first job at age twelve, as a babysitter for the neighbor's children, to yesterday's meetings as a vice president of a company, this manuscript has been forming in my head. With every day that I've gone to work or punched a clock or dealt with an employee problem (including my own); or juggled priorities, rearranged a budget, delegated a duty, had to come in early or stay late, socialized at a company function, or made a career decision, I wrote another mental page.

I didn't know it then, but I've been gathering data since I was a kid. Probably, I've had a businesswoman's mindset all my life, and to tell you the truth, I'm glad. I love networking and brainstorming with others on the firing line of business and commerce. I love taking on risks and difficult projects. I love having an office to call my own. I love being challenged by new ideas and dreams. And I love being "on a team"—it's fun and it keeps me on my toes. It's hard at times, of course, but I believe the benefits far outweigh the drawbacks.

And that's one reason I've written this book. If you are a Christian woman who is in a career—or, more especially, if you would *like* to be in a career—then this book is for you. In it, I want to present a personal view of how you can become a true professional—whatever field you choose—without altering any of your Christian standards or precepts or denying the special gift of your womanhood.

In the pages that follow, I want to suggest a format that works for me and that I feel can work for you—whether you are a college senior anticipating a career, a mother reentering the work force, a recent graduate in an entry-level position, or a veteran who has been on the road awhile but would like to understand a little better where she is going professionally and why.

Let me set a mental stage. At this moment, picture in your mind a road. It has a beginning—where you may be presently standing. And it has an end, a destination—which is probably somewhere out there over the horizon. That destination, which I like to call "your professional niche," is the place where you ultimately want to wind up. It is the fulfillment of your professional dream—the work that is uniquely suited to you.

But this destination is more than just a specific job—even the job of your dreams. It also involves a set of specific characteristics and attitudes—qualities that earmark or distinguish the professional.

In this book, I frequently use the term, "the Christian professional woman," or simply the "professional" woman. But I am using this term in a very specific sense. I am not referring only to the so-called professions—doctors, lawyers, and so forth. And I certainly am not talking about a person who is a professional (as opposed to amateur) at being a woman!

When I use the term "Christian professional woman," I am talking about the Christian woman who sees her work as more than just a job and who goes about it with a thoroughgoing professionalism. (I will talk more about these characteristics in chapter 2.)

Basically, the Christian professional is a person who spends her time building a character, not an empire. There is a vast difference between the two. I believe there are better ways to calculate profit and loss than counting money. What is crucial for true professional fulfillment is not necessarily specialized training nor becoming a power-driven workaholic, but knowing how to think critically, evaluate wisely, and encourage the people who work for and with you.

This is a very important point, because I believe this concept of character and career has been largely neglected in the "career book" market. And the Christian market has had very little to say at all to women who are in careers.

In fact, I've noticed an interesting thing as I've been cognitively researching material for the past three or four years in an effort to bring this book to completion.

There is much written for the working woman who is not a Christian—how to pull rank, how much money to shoot for, who to hobnob with, where to go for lunch and vacation, how to beat the "good-ole-boy" system, and so on. We are told a lot about how to "dress for success," but not much about how to be a successful *human being* in the workplace.

There is also a lot written for the Christian woman who is not a professional—how to put the Lord first in her life and home, how to be happy if she's single, how to have a creative marriage and be submissive to her husband, how to effectively rear her children, and so on.

But I have found very little addressed to the two together—the Christian professional woman who both loves the Lord *and* her work, and who is interested in building her character along with her career.

Not much is written that encourages us to be the best we can be where we are, in our various fields of endeavor or pursuit in the professional world—whether married or unmarried, parent or nonparent, struggling or successful.

Being a Christian woman with a career is a bit of a dichotomy to some folks; they don't quite know what to do with us. They feel that the two worlds of Christianity and professionalism contradict each other where women are concerned—that if you're a Christian, you should not be interested in this world's honors and rewards, and your greatest area of significance should come from your home, family, and church.

I find that viewpoint shortsighted and narrow. If you are a businesswoman, performer, sportswoman, entrepreneur, leader in any field, there is a world of opportunity to utilize and convey Christian principles in the workplace.

It's a challenge like no other. There are never-ending occasions to witness, help, care, give, understand, be involved with people who desperately need to be encouraged and loved as they are. As Christian career women, our greatest calling is to love people, to line up our causes within the overall cause of Christ and allow Him to use us to effect meaningful changes in the lives of those around us. The journey to our professional niche is one of the most exciting spiritual adventures life has to offer.

This book is about how to get there from here.

chapter one

The
Wandering

The content of the job is largely irrelevant. The point is to experience . . .

—RICHARD BOLLES
The Three Boxes of Life

GAIL COX had gone for an easy one-hour hike in the woods. Dressed in a bathing suit with caftan and wearing tennis shoes, she set out on a hot Monday morning to see the wildflowers at nearby Stoddard Lake. And although the trail was rougher and more indistinct than she expected, Gail was so entranced by the beauty around her—the shimmering lake, a snowcapped peak, the carpet of flowers—that she stopped noticing whether she was on the trodden path. As a result, when she started back to her vacation cabin later that afternoon, she found herself far from the trail.

At first Gail was more annoyed than alarmed, but she became more uneasy when her wandering continued. The terrain turned steeper and more treacherous. A sodden meadow pulled at her tennis shoes. She fell—rolled down a hill and finally stopped herself with her walking stick.

"This is ridiculous," she thought. "This is an hour's walk. What's wrong with me? Where's the trail?"

Gail Cox was a newspaper reporter, respected by her co-workers for her common sense, her remarkable memory, and her quick wit. At forty, she had learned to be self-reliant, so no one had been particularly surprised when she decided to vacation alone at a retreat in California's rugged Trinity Alps. But now Gail was beginning to doubt the wisdom of the trip.

After a few hours of stumbling through the underbrush, Gail Cox had to admit to herself, "I am definitely lost. And I have been doing everything wrong, and people who are lost panic and go in circles and die." But Gail was determined not to die, so she slowed down and took stock of her situation.

Gail determined she was most in danger of heat exhaustion, dehydration, breaking an ankle, hitting her head, and having her tennis shoes fall apart. Less likely were snakes and hypothermia. And too remote to bother with were bears, starvation, maniacs, lightning, and ghosts.

It was becoming clear that she would probably have to spend the night in the woods. But at daybreak, she decided, she'd hike down to a nearby stream and wait for a rescue team—which she was sure would be dispatched when she failed to return to her cabin.

To sleep, Gail curled up on the ground and used her purse and shoes for a pillow. When she heard rustling in the bushes, she said, "Go away," in a firm voice, and the rustling stopped.

At dawn Tuesday, she found an old press release in her purse and wrote a note saying she was unhurt, "if you discount my acute embarrassment at the problem I'm causing."

There was no rescue Tuesday, although she saw a white helicopter flying away from her over a ridge. On Wednesday morning, she decided to follow the stream, which ran down a rocky gorge filled with boulders and fallen trees. When the banks became impassable, she walked down the middle until she hit rapids or waterfalls. All along, she left little piles of stones as signs for the rescuers.

Late Wednesday afternoon, Gail came upon a small, level clearing with a pile of decaying firewood and a rusted beer can. Relieved at that sign of human life, she lay down and soon was asleep.

Thursday morning she awoke to the dying sound of a low-flying helicopter over the opposite ridge. Desperately she raced around the campsite, gathering dry pine needles to start a fire and signal rescuers. But the helicopter was gone by the time the needles finally caught.

At that point, Gail determined that helping herself

was even more important than trying to notify rescuers. So she began to make some decisions. Amazingly enough, she found that the decision-making process itself boosted her spirits. Whether her decisions were right or wrong at this point didn't matter. At least there was a feeling of being in control.

Gail decided to spend all of Thursday at her newfound campsite recuperating—and without question, she needed the rest! By now there was a knot on her left shin, a large purple bruise on her calf, and a cut on her leg. Her lips were swollen and cracked, her big toe was scraped, her shoulders were completely covered with insect bites. So she rested. This helped. She also discovered that if she carefully tended the fire she could sleep an hour at a stretch all through the day and night.

Friday morning, she washed her clothes in the river. She put on the wet swimsuit and had just finished drying her caftan over the fire when a man's voice startled her: "Hello there." Turning, she saw a young man carrying a creel and fishing pole.

"I've been lost out here since Monday by myself," Gail managed to croak, "and I am very glad to see you."

Gail Cox was later told by rescuers that she'd done all the right things to save herself. And she returned from her days of wandering more or less unscathed. She claims there are lessons she learned from her experience that she will never forget.

For one thing, before she discards something as insignificant as a paper towel, she asks herself, "Is this something I might need?"

She also marvels at the luxuries we all take for granted, such as being able to get a drink of water without having to lie on her stomach.

And Gail is much more conscious of her own mortality. The day after her rescue, a young Army reservist with survival training and experience in the mountains was reported missing in the same area where Gail had been lost. His body was found six days later at the base of a cliff!

Today Gail Cox finds herself telling people, "When you're lost in the mountains, you can either stay in one place and wait for the searchers, or you can wander around and take action to save yourself. The first way enhances your chances of being rescued. The second enhances your whole life."[1]

Nobody likes to be lost. It's a terrible, scary feeling. There's panic and fear and bewilderment and confusion and much wandering around to find a way out of the maze.

The very definition of "lost" is thoroughly negative. "Not spent profitably or usefully; wasted; attended with defeat." That's what the dictionary tells us.

Nevertheless, Gail Cox, who was lost and wandering for five days in the wilderness, reports that during that time she learned lessons about life she could not have learned otherwise—lessons that helped to shape her future.

But how does her story help us?

At the very start of this book I compared the professional journey to a road with a beginning and an end—the end being your professional niche. But the truth is that we don't always get on that road right away. Many of us spend "lost" time wandering around before we get going.

And it's right there that we get hung up. We become discouraged because we can't seem to get off the dime. We've graduated from school, we've planned our future, our kids are grown—whatever. We simply need to get going, we feel. Pronto! We have the attitude that if we don't charge out like a race car in the Indy 500, leading the pack, we're a failure. We visualize any wandering from the direct route as without value.

Of course, that's not true for everyone, I realize. Some women know from their youngest years exactly what they want in terms of a career, and with clear and singular goals in mind they follow their dream toward fulfillment. That happens, although I believe it's rare.

Other women have careers thrust upon them by circumstances—having to be the breadwinner because of an illness, divorce, or death of a spouse; having inherited a leadership responsibility they did not voluntarily choose; having enlisted their services in an activity that started out small and grew into a big-time operation. These people, too, may start on their path without too much wandering.

But for most of us, the career path begins in a rather nebulous way. One door opens that we find appealing, so we walk through it. Then another door opens, somewhat off the trodden way, and we walk through it, too, because we feel it will add to our knowledge or advancement or both. Later, perhaps realizing that neither of these doors opened to vistas that provided the satisfaction or fulfillment we were looking for, we resign those positions and try something else.

All the while, there may be a hazy goal on the horizon of our minds, but it is so far away that we can't be absolutely sure it is always there or *really* what we want—it comes and goes. So we rabbit-trail, for years sometimes, in search of that ideal career or job that will provide the ultimate attainment we sought in life.

Many people call this period of time their "lost years"—the years without value or gain, the years when "I could have accomplished something but didn't." Consequently, these years are often viewed with regret or disappointment.

I differ. I call such a period "the wandering," and I believe it can be the most important and profitable time of anyone's life. The information gathered and the lessons learned during this interval are relevant to the rest of our careers—and, more importantly, the rest of our lives.

At the most basic level, this time of dead ends, false leads, and entry-level work points us toward experience. We may not be on the career road yet, but for many of us this is the time when we are first exposed to some of the artifacts of the working world—being on time, handling money, taking orders, relating to other people, enduring discipline, finishing a task, and so on. Again, these are extremely basic lessons, but there's simply no way to achieve your professional niche without learning them.

The time of wandering can also teach us some important lessons about what we *don't* want—what's not right for us. And these negative lessons, too, can be valuable in keeping us on the right professional road later on.

How long we wander around before getting on the path that leads to our professional niche depends on many factors. Some people settle into their workplace and their career niche very quickly; others of us wander a great deal.

It certainly took me awhile to get moving in a clear direction! Not long ago, just for fun, I made a list of all the jobs I have held since I began working some forty-two years ago, as a babysitter, at the age of twelve. At each of these posts, I actually was receiving payment for my duties. They are listed in the order they occurred, with a few overlaps:

- Babysitter
- Lawn Maintenance Helper
- Door-to-door Magazine Salesperson
- Salesperson in a Variety Store
- Salesperson in a Department Store
- Summer Camp Staff Worker
- Traveling "Vacation Bible School" Planner
- Waitress
- Swimming Instructor
- Teacher
- Chorister
- Soloist
- Union Rep for AGMA (American Guild of Musical Artists)
- Traveling Rep for a College
- Artist

- Greeting Card Designer
- China Painter
- Draftsman
- Technical Illustrator
- Radio/TV Guest
- Rights of Way Agent
- Manager of Rights of Way Department for oil company
- Editor
- Speaker
- Author
- Vice President of Public Relations

As you can see, I did quite a lot of "miscellaneous" work before developing any kind of meaningful career. During all this wandering, there were occasions I felt defeated or lost. I often asked myself, "What is going to become of me? What do I really want to do with my life? How can I ever get ahead or make any money if I don't settle into something permanent?"

There were other occasions when I could feel myself on a journey, (on a "role," in a sense). But I couldn't imagine where I was headed. Little did I realize that beneath the frustrations and anxieties of my seemingly haphazard career, something *was* happening. Willy-nilly, in order or out of order, I was learning how to cope with life's demands and deal with the issues that face each of us in our career pursuits.

In many (I would say most) instances, I was too young to see it; therefore the benefits from my wandering years did not come to me except in retrospect. That's unfortunate because each job I held taught me something about a job that was yet to come, but because of my own eagerness to move ahead or dissatisfaction with the duties at present, I couldn't perceive that the truths and lessons I was learning were going to benefit me for a lifetime.

Almost everything I learned in those early jobs proved

of value as building blocks for later professional success. But the essentials were not clarified in my mind until some five or ten years ago. (My own wandering occurred when I was much younger, but some women experience it later in life, particularly when they are starting out in a new career direction. Lessons learned, however, can be valuable at any age.)

I used to feel that since much of what I learned about work and my career resulted from wandering around without a conscious direction, it was largely unusable and unsystematizable—devoid of organizing principles. But I was wrong. I felt that much of my life had been wasted, but I was wrong.

So if you are on that same merry-go-round or live with the mindset of defeat because you haven't found your professional niche yet, cheer up. There's hope in these organizing principles, based on Gail Cox's experience in the mountains:

Principle #1:
DON'T DISCARD YOUR SCRAPS

First, before you discard any information or tidbits of wisdom as insignificant or useless, ask yourself, "Is this something I might need?"

I have a friend living in Seattle who is a perfect example of what I'm trying to say. Her name is Lynda Austin. A bright, charming Christian girl, Lynda is a college graduate with a degree in communications, yet so far she has been unable to get on the right road to her professional niche. In a recent letter, she made reference to this uncertain period in her life. With her permission, I share that portion of her letter with you:

> Cognitively, I see the value in these years I have spent wandering. I've learned so many important lessons one cannot learn in a book or even in school. My dad teases me

26

about graduating from college only to enter the school of hard knocks. That's for sure! It has always been comforting to remember hearing you say that you wouldn't re-live your twenties for anything . . . I only have three more years to go, and I can honestly say things are getting better.

One of the best things I've done was decide to get out of debt. The number one piece of advice I would have for those in their wandering years is not to wander too far with only credit cards in your pocket! Especially if you don't have a stable job or stable career goals. I am learning a very hard lesson about credit but I guess it's better to learn it now and take care of my debts than learn it in twenty years with twenty times the dollar amount. Of course, I'm not out of the woods yet, but I'm on my way.

I've decided another good thing to do while wandering is work through all the confusion, anger, hurt, whatever— you have toward your parents, childhood, church, etc. and leave that baggage on the road somewhere on your travels. Then, when you decide to settle down in a permanent relationship and/or career, all these unsettled issues won't come back to haunt you without your previously having battled them on your own.

Thank you Lynda. That's excellent advice. Where were you when I needed to know that in *my* twenties?

Look for a minute at some well-known professional newspaper columnists who have admitted to "saving the scraps" of their experiences. Erma Bombeck confesses that she "had no goals whatsoever" when she began writing a column for a suburban Ohio newspaper. But her subjects—kids and carpools, what Lily Tomlin used to call the world of meatballs and mending—wound up netting her a minimum of $500,000 annually just because she never regarded the vignettes of her life as insignificant.

Or Ellen Goodman, that crusader of the *Boston Globe* who tracks social change and reports the process. Unlike a lot of columnists, who make use of assistants to scout ideas and clip newspapers, Ms. Goodman chooses her own subjects and does her own research. She does this because no one else knows what she's looking for. "It's mysterious," she says. "I'm collecting string all the time." The smallest scrap of news or information might become the basis for a column.

Or, there's Bea Hines, the 47-year-old black writer for the *Miami Herald* who says it's her "responsibility to be a watchperson for people who can't fight for themselves." Widowed in 1964 with two young sons, Hines, then a maid, answered every ad in the newspaper that said, "Equal Opportunity Employer." She was finally hired at the *Herald* as a file clerk for sixty dollars a week—ten dollars more than she was making as a maid. In time, she worked up to being a staff reporter. But she acknowledges now that her experience as a maid taught her more about all kinds of people than she could ever learn as a reporter.[2] She has been able to use those scraps of her early experience to build a completely different kind of career.

In July 1986, *Working Woman* published an interesting article entitled "Designing A Corporate Image."[3] It was the story of Anne Breckenridge, who is presently responsible for maintaining the interior-design image of a $7.36 billion company in Atlanta, Georgia.

The article points out that Ms. Breckenridge's present job is the first corporate position she has held after a career path that took her through more than a half-dozen jobs and four states in twenty-five years. "When I started out," she acknowledges in the article, "my basic plan was to get married, work for a few years and have a baby. But then I got the biggest shock of my life—I found out that this dream doesn't happen for everybody. My husband and I divorced when our daughter was two years old."

Ms. Breckenridge tells about enrolling at Berkeley's College of Environmental Design to get an M.A. in design—with only a ten-year-old B.A. from the University of Colorado. After graduation she was hired as a junior designer at an architectural firm, only to have her experience there lead her to a better job in another state. "I've suffered several setbacks," Breckenridge tells us. "The job in Florida turned out to be a real dead end. Later, in a recession, I was laid off by a design firm."

But the cream of the article that surfaced above everything else was this line: "It's important to remember that rising to a great place is often—or usually—by a winding staircase."

Anne Breckenridge calls it "a winding staircase." I call it "the wandering"—but it's the same thing. It's the circuitous path that finally leads us to the main road toward our professional niche. And the first principle of getting there is never to discard as insignificant any information along the path.

Principle #2:
DON'T LOSE YOUR WONDER

The second thing Gail Cox learned from her time of wandering was to "marvel at the luxuries we all take for granted." And that, too, is a good principle for the wandering times in our professional lives.

Each of us is surrounded by opportunities to become excited and involved in activities at hand. But we're waiting for the other shoe to drop. We're wanting things to get better, to lighten up, to go away. We're waiting for a ship to come in that never went out.

During our months or years of wandering we need to appreciate what is "now." So what if we go down a false road or two along the way, or spend some time in a "dead-end job" as Anne Breckenridge calls it? It's not the end of the world—we can backtrack and go on from there. But we must never lose our sense of marvel, appreciation, and wonder. I believe this period of time gives opportunity for our hearts to expand. It's a chance to examine not only what we think about work, but how we feel about what we're doing and where we're heading.

The women who allow themselves to feel they are pursuing a wonderful career (or better stated, a career full of wonder), more often than not end up finding the niche they want, laboring at what they love—even when everything is not always logical or reasonable. They're the ones whose characters, not the demands of their empires, dictate their efforts. And they're the ones who find that underlying sense of purpose that is foundational to most human happiness. Wonder enlarges our vision and our efforts.

This period of wandering and searching, however, should be a time for intellectual enthusiasm, an opportunity to conduct friendly debates with those who view the world differently. Overall, it should be a time of learning to enjoy the life of the mind and the spirit, rather than having to simply tolerate what one doesn't find interesting.

Principle #3:
REMEMBER YOUR OWN MORTALITY

The third principle says a period of wandering causes one to become more profoundly conscious of the impermanence of life on this earth. There is something in the very act of wandering that shows us we are mortal, that nothing within us—the happiness and pain, the light and the dark, the cheerfulness of childhood or the apprehension of death, settles into permanency on this earth. We are always only a moment away from the possibility of eternity itself.

Life has no guarantee that tomorrow we will still be here. Therefore, we should say yes to the avenues that beckon us, even when we cannot clearly see where they are going. There are lessons to be learned that we can learn no other way.

A wandering period can be a very real time of prayer, trust, and faith in God—that He will provide, protect and guide us into the exact place He wants to put us for our greatest development and outreach.

The Wandering

Wandering is an uncertain time, but it can be very meaningful. Many of life's deepest blessings are hidden in uncertainties, which too often we shy away from.

Be sure of this: the wanderer is different from the person who remains at home. She tends to love more deeply and to be more aware of the gift of God's provision at every turn.

The wanderer is a richer person. Although she may not have found the route yet, she is on her way.

chapter two

The
Route

I am saying that both the destination and the route should be considered, and both should be interesting. We spend a great deal more time on the road than we do at the destination. Therefore, pick the best road, which isn't always the fastest. Learn how to enjoy the whole trip, the road as well as the goal.

—FRED SMITH
You and Your Network

WITH THE PERIOD of wandering behind us, and armed with the knowledge and skills learned during those years, we come to a time when our objectives must be carefully defined. In order to move forward toward our aspirations, we must ask and answer several questions of ourselves— questions like, What *is* a career woman anyway? What does she look and act like? How did she get where she is? Can *I* ever arrive at that destination? We must know where we want to go and what we want to do when we get there.

Consider our target: the professional Christian woman. You and I may not agree on every nitty-gritty element, but we need a broad definition toward which to aim. How about this: The professional woman is the experienced individual whose work displays exceptional quality, not only of achievement, but of character and conduct. She is definitely not an amateur!

Added to that, this woman is one who can be counted on under virtually any conditions. She's not afraid of hard work; she treats other people the way she wants to be treated; and she works this way year-in and year-out. A true professional is not petty and doesn't give up easily.

I must come back to that basic thought I referred to in the prologue, because it is the key to this book: A professional woman is the person who has her sights not on building an empire, but on building a character.

There are three well-known women whose lives I have observed with interest for a number of years. Each is over fifty, and each possesses the attributes that I believe characterize a true professional. I have watched them from afar with admiration and respect and have, on occasion, sought to emulate their style and demeanor. I've read their books and gleaned much wisdom from their writings. The first woman is Beverly Sills, the opera singer turned entrepreneur; the second, a New York model named Kaylan Pickford; and the third, Sophia Loren, that stunning Italian beauty who never seems to age.

What is it these women have that made them successful professionals and keeps them at the top of the ladder? What was the route they took that brought them to the pinnacle of achievement? What are their secrets?

I believe there are four elements vital to professional success and achievement. But before listing them, I should add that there is a distinction between success and achievement.

As Helen Hayes's mother once told her, "Achievement is the knowledge that you have studied and worked hard and done the best that is in you. Success is being praised by others, and that's nice too, but not as important or satisfying. Always aim for achievement and forget about success." Good advice!

What are the four elements that lead to professional success? I believe that a true professional must have brains, courage, heart, and faith. These elements pave the road to the building of character. They are absolutely fundamental. The longer I live and the more I am around professional people, the more I see these qualities manifesting themselves over and over.

Now, I've known empire builders with only brains or courage, but they don't embody enough character for me to call them professionals. They are often cold, shallow, avaricious, lonely persons whom I pity rather than admire. They may be prosperous, but to me they aren't professionals.

I've also known individuals who are all heart, with tremendous gifts of generosity, compassion, courtesy, and kindness, but who lack a willingness to change or take a risk, so they never really move on to their goal. They're too busy pleasing everyone.

Or, there's the person who is locked into the idea of faith, but without work—never putting the pedal to the metal. No action. No growth. No fruit.

The secret is achieving the balance of all these elements. In truly professional women, these characteristics overlap. You cannot tell where one ends and the other begins.

Element #1:
BRAINS

Take Beverly Sills. The woman has brains! I'm not saying that one must be an intellectual giant to qualify for professional status. I'm also not claiming that a college education is necessary to do well in life, although I personally feel a degree opens certain doors that cannot be opened otherwise. A liberal arts education does wonders to give us a taste of the varied world of knowledge, but it isn't mandatory for being professional. Countless women are pros who never got a college diploma. Beverly Sills is one. When I say she has brains, I mean she is an example of one who never stops learning. And she uses her head—all the time.

At three years of age, Beverly Sills was singing. By the time she was ten she was speaking French and Italian, as well as taking piano and singing lessons. She learned classical guitar. She sang commercials and jingles, all the while avidly reading the classics and studying opera roles. By the age of twenty-three she had learned one hundred operas. Beverly Sills had a purpose. She dreamed of being an opera star, and she used her head to pursue this dream all her life.

It's good to have dreams. Dreams are motivating. They give us purpose and direction. They help us set goals, and of course goals are vital for the professional woman. But I don't list dreaming as one of the basic elements of professionalism because if we don't use our heads, our courage, our hearts, and our faith to put them into motion, that's all they are—dreams, a mental list of objectives to achieve.

Personally, I am very goal-oriented. I operate best in a goal-oriented, structured environment because it has order and I like order. Things without order depress me, pull my spirit down, and consequently, I don't produce. Lack of order saps my energy. But that's me. That may not be you, and you may still achieve professional success. I have a friend—an extremely professional high achiever—who never sets goals. She operates out of her hip pocket, and that seems to work for her. But she does have brains . . . and oh, how she uses them! That's why I believe that continuing to learn, using our heads, expanding our horizons are even more important than setting goals.

Beverly Sills is the recipient of five honorary degrees. The citation for the doctorate she received from Harvard in 1974 read:

> Her joyous personality, glorious voice, and deep knowledge of music and drama bring delight to her audiences and distinction to her art.[1]

What a compliment to pay to someone! These comments are directed to one who has more than classroom or book knowledge—much more. They are the recognition of an individual who has applied herself to every phase of growth and learning. Her art is the radiant outpouring of her inner life and character.

Ms. Sills has never stopped growing and developing even under the agony of family heartaches. She and her husband, Peter Greenough, have two handicapped children. Their daughter, Muffy, was diagnosed as deaf at the age of twenty-three months. Their son, Bucky, is mentally retarded; this was discovered when he was two months old.

Many women would let the anguish of even one of these heartaches wipe out all desire to go on. But not Beverly Sills. She claims that she found a "kind of serenity, a new maturity" as a result of her children's problems. Her singing voice changed—became more enriched, more enriching. Her own comments convey her feelings:

> Instead of using my singing just to build a career. . . . I began singing for pure pleasure. I was singing not because I wanted to be Beverly Sills Superstar, but because I needed to sing—desperately. My voice poured out more easily because I was no longer singing for anyone's approval; I was beyond caring about the public's reaction, I just wanted to enjoy myself . . . I didn't feel better or stronger than anyone else but it seemed no longer important whether everyone loved me or not—more important now was for me to love them. Feeling that way turns your whole life around: living becomes the act of giving. When I do a performance now, I still need and like the adulation of an audience, of course, but my *real* satisfaction comes from what I have given of myself, from the joyful act of singing itself.[2]

Is that not precisely what Helen Hayes's mother told her was the distinction between success and achievement?

Beverly Sills is no longer performing on the operatic stage, but is the guiding force behind the New York City Opera—to international laurels. Her interest in and love of opera never stop. And she keeps on growing even today. She comments, "I no longer have to do anything professionally or personally that I don't want to do. And as long as I am having a good time, I don't intend to stop."[3]

Don't ever stop growing! Keep using your head. Keep learning. The real obstacles to growth seem to be within ourselves. It is our responsibility to determine how we will spend our days. Will they be spent in living fully or dying slowly?

Often we find ourselves terrified at the turmoils of human life—we want to stop the world and get off. I've said before that if there were just a little booth attached to the side of the world where I could go and sit and think and pray and wait until this or that problem is over, I'd be so much happier. Then, when I was better and stronger, I'd come back into real life.

But it doesn't work that way. And if it did, I'd never grow. I'd never learn. The way I learn is in the *midst* of the turmoil, because it's not the little booth that calls out my resourceful best; it's the turmoil. Difficult times give me spiritual insight and a chance to trust God, even though that certainly may not be my choice. They pave my way toward endurance, focus, responsibility . . . and courage.

Element #2:
COURAGE

Courage. Here's the second element that is foundational to professionalism. In late 1983, I ran across a most interesting-looking book called *Always A Woman*, by Kaylan Pickford. On the front of the book, under Ms. Pickford's name, were these lines:

Always . . . the greatest beauty is inner beauty . . .

Always . . . life is worth living and celebrating.

My philosophy in a nutshell—so I bought the book in a flash!

Also on the cover was a colored photo of the loveliest gray-haired woman with a contented, happy look on her face—Kaylan Pickford. I liked her clothes. I liked her smile and I *loved* the book. I read it the day I bought it, and that night I wrote Ms. Pickford a letter, congratulating her on her insightful writing. (This is something I often say I must do after reading a good book, but rarely do it because of lack of time. In this case I did it, and I'm so glad.) In a couple of weeks she responded with a very kind message of encouragement and appreciation. Needless to say, I was thrilled.

Ms. Pickford is a fascinating woman. Out of intense experiences of love and tragedy and the rebuilding of a shattered life, she gives us an exciting account of what can happen when a person lays her life on the line and has the courage to take a risk. She tells us the painful truth of how she learned to make decisions.

After ten years of marriage that produced two daughters, Ms. Pickford was divorced. Her second marriage also ended in misfortune. Two weeks home from her honeymoon, and only a month following the wedding to a husband she adored, he was diagnosed with cancer. Four and a half years later, after a long and painful struggle for his life, he died on New Year's Eve, 1968. Kaylan Pickford was a widow at thirty-eight.

Alone, lonely, unskilled and grief-stricken, Kaylan had no vision, no direction, so she withdrew. "In time I accepted the truth that my life would not change until I changed it. I recognized that everything I had learned and had come to understand would be meaningless if I failed to use myself. I needed to let go of inner pain, to move into life. I needed to work."[4]

Through the years, Ms. Pickford had always taken care of her personal appearance. Looking good was part of her armor to sustain a sense of well-being when times were difficult. She always wanted to maintain a vibrant physical appearance in order to project an inner strength that was reassuring to her husband and children. She claims that this not only enabled her to establish a discipline and healthy attitude when she found herself living alone after her children were grown and her husband gone; but also served as the catalyst that caused her, without references or guidance, to blindly and naïvely make her way into the modeling world.

She began at the age of forty-five, when everyone told her she would fail. They said an older woman would not have the vitality or the appeal of a younger woman. They were wrong. Today she is one of the nation's most photographed women and a leading New York model. That transition began with courage.

Courage is another way of saying "take a risk." Believe me, it is *impossible* to become a professional woman in today's world without risk taking. Once we determine what we hope to become, aligning our goals with our values, then we must put courage in gear to get the vehicle moving down the road.

"Experience is the child born of risk," says Ms. Pickford. "Any degree of risk has some element of the unknown, but no one courts risk without believing that there is some chance to achieve what they set out to do."[5]

Earlier this year I read *America's New Women Entrepreneurs: Tips, Tactics and Techniques of Women Achievers in Business.* The book was a gift from a friend I admire greatly, Dale Hanson Bourke, president of Publishing Directions, Inc. and senior editor of *Today's Christian Woman.* The book is the compilation of comments from thirty-two of America's foremost women achievers. These are women from every business under the sun: sports, cosmetics, realty, marketing, home interiors, finance, publishing, foods, advertising, fabrics—you name it! In the book, each woman gives a brief summary of how she rose to success and prosperity, overcoming odds and roadblocks, and closes her chapter with "Tips for Success." What interesting lists! I found myself making my own list of tips as I read theirs. Each woman's ideas were born out of her own circumstances in how she got ahead, and each, I'm sure, has personal value.

But, here's what was so exciting to me as I read all those tips: Out of the thirty-two women who expressed their ideas for achievement, nineteen spoke about the necessity of taking risks, being willing to change. Not being afraid to make mistakes, seizing opportunities. Courage.

One thing in particular Kaylan Pickford said which I found beneficial was this: "When people hear things that suggest changes in their lives, their comfort, they resist what they hear and therefore the person saying it. Only when we become committed to what we want to accomplish

will change occur. We make it happen when we take responsibility for our own lives."[6]

How true, how true! But again, we must know where
we're going before we can ever get on the route.

I so well remember driving to work one hot July morning in 1981, on a busy, packed Los Angeles freeway. I was
praying, "Lord, I'd like to do something significant with
my life. I've been with Mobil for about twenty-five years,
and while I'm not bored, I'd like something really exciting
and challenging to fall across my horizon. Something I
can do to help people. And Lord, let me know when it
happens because I don't want to miss the blessing—the
fun." (Being of the conviction that often we miss the deepest joy of our prayer life because we haven't asked God to
show us when we're there, I occasionally tag that last part
on my prayers.)

That evening I was at a party at the home of my brother
and his wife, Chuck and Cynthia Swindoll, who were enter-
taining the staff of Multnomah Press. The Multnomah
people were in the Los Angeles area for the 1981 Christian Booksellers Association Convention in Anaheim. Everyone was having a jolly old time swimming, chatting,
eating, laughing—the usual fare at the Swindolls'—but as
we neared the end of the party, Multnomah's publisher,
John Van Diest, asked if I would stay a few minutes after-
wards. He wanted to talk with me about something.

When all the other guests had drifted out the door,
John, Chuck, Cynthia, and I sat sipping our last cup of
coffee. John said, "Luci, have you ever thought about writing a book?"

"No."

"Would you be interested in writing a book on the single
life for Multnomah Press? Chuck tells me you've been single by choice all your life. Is that true?"

"True."

"Well, how about it? Want to write a book for us?"

I was stunned. While the idea of writing a book had,

admittedly, flashed into my mind once or twice because I've always kept journals and loved writing letters, I had never seriously considered doing it. No sooner would the thought appear than I would scare it away with, "Are you nuts, Luci? What would you say in a book? Forget it."

But do you know what happened when John presented me with that idea? It was the strangest thing. My prayer of that morning returned crystal clear to my mind, and I kept seeing the word *significant* flash off and on in my mind's eye like a neon sign on the side of an old hotel. Significant. Significant.

"Naw, Lord. You can't mean *this*. I can't do this."

Then, just as clearly, the sign flashed, "Do it. This is it, you jerk. You prayed about this, now *do* it."

So, in spite of my fears, excuses, and disbelief, I heard myself saying to John, "Okay. I'll try."

Those three words changed so many things about my life. I did write the book on the single life. And one after that on freedom, and another after that on celebration. Then a fourth on God's constancy, and now this one on the professional journey. And there will probably be others, since I never know when to quit!

Since I've been writing books, *countless* doors have opened. I have had speaking engagements all over the nation, cruises, radio interviews, television appearances. There have been hundreds of opportunities to talk with people about their careers, their lives, their problems, their relationships, their hopes, and most importantly, the new way of life offered in Jesus Christ. I've made new friends and had reunions with old friends . . . some of whom have appeared out of the woodwork—people I thought I'd never see again and often wondered where they were. Gosh, it's been wonderful! And on and on it goes. *Because I took a risk.* Because I said, "Okay, I'll try"— three little words but with such big dividends.

With this example, look for a moment at some of the byproducts of courage and how they tie in to our definition of the professional woman. Remember, Kaylan Pickford said, "Experience is the child of risk." There's no doubt about it—I've gained a world of experience by accepting Mr. Van Diest's challenge to write a book. I like to think my writing has also improved. Even my business letters in my work reflect improvement from the experience of writing books and speeches. (Maybe they've turned into novels and no one has the heart to tell me. A writer does run that chance.) My spelling has surely improved, which didn't take much.

Whenever we travel we gain experience. Remember, in the last chapter I said that the person who leaves home becomes a richer person. We gain experience as we meet new people, expanding our horizons with new ideas, new ways of looking at life, new ways of dealing with problems and people, new ways of setting priorities.

The actual achievement of writing a book built my confidence, too. You think I'm not scared at times that I won't finish, or that I don't have the right stuff or have bitten off more than I can chew? Of course I'm scared. Those feelings come in like a flood some days. For two cents I'd throw in the towel—if I knew where to throw it. With writing there are so many unknowns and feelings of inadequacy. But I am "in it," with a signed book contract, and I know enough about contracts from my days at Mobil to realize I can't get out of one lightly. Besides, I am determined to finish the manuscript even if it never gets into print, thank you!

So, little by little, page by page, chapter by chapter, it adds up—just as this one is doing. And one day, zappo! There it is—a book. A real, bound, completed book. My book. That's the best part. *My book.* Each time I look at a book I've written, it says so much more to me than the physical object itself. It says sacrifice and work and rewrites and late nights and early mornings and love and courage and vulnerability—all those things, those qualities that make anything of value what it is.

Each time I am invited to work on a new manuscript I go through the same mental rigamarole: "Well, if I did it once, why not try again? That was fun—well, sorta fun. There were tough times, but so what? There would be tough times even if I sat here doing nothing but letting mold form on my body. I'd rather be in there making a difference to somebody."

Then I'm off again on another challenge, but I am stronger and more confident because I have a bit of history to back me up.

The road to professionalism is not a well-marked super-highway that we traverse in the world's sleekest, hottest, latest problem-free sports car. No . . . the road to professionalism has accidents on it and roadblocks and detours. Sometimes we're a part of those things, but we don't spend the rest of our lives there in the middle of them. We don't give up and lie down by the side of the road and say, "I'm finished, folks. Count me out. I'm not going any farther because here's a roadblock, or here's an accident." Of course not! We look for ways to circumvent these situations that slow us down. We take care of the problem and move on. Perhaps we proceed a bit more cautiously at first, but don't worry, we'll soon pick up speed!

Courage enables us to live on life's exciting edge. It produces a heightened awareness and an appetite for living fully. It keeps us wondering what's going to happen next.

The peculiar thing about taking risks as opposed to not taking them is that there seems to be no middle ground. They are poles apart.

Let me explain. Most of us hate change; we fight it tooth and nail. We find every excuse in the book to avoid taking a risk because risk-taking forces us out of our comfort zone. We ask a million "what ifs": What if it isn't safe? What if we lose all our money? What if others aren't pleased? What if we bomb? What if we overestimate our abilities? What if "they" find out we're really faking it? (The royal *they* I call it, because nobody knows who "they" are, up in that mighty tower above us, and "they" are probably looking at "us" saying, "Who are they?")

So ominous is the threat of change that we submit to tedium, boredom, and apathy—then what happens? We feel trapped. We're in a rut. Life is a grind. We hate ourselves and our circumstances. I've heard those comments over and over and over from people who want to move ahead, yet wonder why they don't. They are scared to death of risk.

Don't live your life in fear. Have courage. Desire to change your circumstances, then get at it. The philosopher Descartes wrote, "Desire awakens only to things that are thought possible." Our characters simply cannot develop until we are willing to be courageous in our circumstances. Stop holding back!

Kaylan Pickford ends her book with the line, "I risked therefore I have." When you reach the day you no longer ignore the inner prompting, when you listen to the whisper that tells you to change, to stretch higher, to learn something new, to alter your attitude—do it. Today is that day!

Element #3:
HEART

Let's talk about heart.

As an executive with Insight for Living, I use what I call The Wizard of Oz approach to management: Use your brain, have the courage to take a risk, but most of all, have a heart. In other words, don't be afraid to be nice.

That may sound somewhat empty at first because it's a phrase we've all heard from childhood. Remember your mother saying, "Now when the company comes, *please* be nice." (At least I heard it often in my household!)

But what does "be nice" mean? What does it mean to have a heart?

Simply put, having a heart means caring about other people. It means motivating instead of manipulating; being a nurturing facilitator instead of a hovering parent; being positive instead of negative, supportive instead of critical, enthusiastic instead of pessimistic; communicating the good news instead of calculating the bad. A professional woman with heart is a person who advocates vulnerability rather than invincibility. She is not afraid to be wrong and say so. She gives credit where it's due. She's a team player who exhibits respect and appreciation without fear of feeling diminished.

Next to my desk at the office I have two quotations stuck on the wall that were clipped from a publication called *Successful Supervisor*. (That's a bulletin that floated around the building while I was at Mobil; it was full of inspirational tidbits for those who manage people.) I want to pass them both on to you because I think they are well worth remembering and applying in our lives.

First, "Good supervision is a matter of technique, but great supervision is a matter of character. The greater your maturity and spiritual stature, the less likely you are to think of yourself, and the more likely you are to think of others, stressing the best that is in them. You get real results!"—E. F. Wells.[7]

The second piece is called "I Will Do More," by William Arthur Ward.

> I will do more than belong.
>> I will *participate*.
> I will do more than care.
>> I will *help*.
> I will do more than believe.
>> I will be *kind*.
> I will do more than forgive.
>> I will *forget*.
> I will do more than dream.
>> I will *work*.
> I will do more than teach.
>> I will *inspire*.
> I will do more than earn.

I will *enrich.*
I will do more than give.
I will *serve.*
I will do more than live.
I will *grow.*
I will do more than be friendly.
I will be a *friend.*
I will do more than be a citizen.
I will be a *patriot.* [8]

Aren't those great? Truly they are goals to aim for, and many can be reached if we simply apply our hearts to life's situations.

The concept of heart becomes especially crucial when it applies to women in management positions. I have worked with a number of women managers/supervisors and talked with numerous others who feel that a boss cannot be effective unless she throws her weight around, barking out orders and lording it over her subordinates. Simply because she has the power of position or a title, she feels she must use it like an iron club.

But this is almost never effective in terms of getting the job done. People are rarely motivated by force. Oh, they may complete the task at hand and produce under the gun, but they'll bad-mouth the manager all the way along and find every available opportunity to undermine her efforts. The truth is they'll hate her guts! She'll be invincible, but who gives a hoot? That kind of management says a lot more negatives about her than it does about the people who work for her. Plus, it simply doesn't work.

I firmly believe you can convey any message gently— even if it is the worst news in the world, if you know how to say it. It's not *what* is said, but *how* it is said, that is important. Put yourself in the other person's shoes. The professional manager is a coach, a teacher, a mentor, and it would behoove many an aspiring professional woman to remember that fact, Christian or not.

If you are in a management position, are you a boss or a

leader? The boss inspires fear; the leader inspires eagerness. The boss says, "I"; the leader says, "We." The boss sees only today; the leader also looks at tomorrow. The boss is concerned with things; the leader is concerned with people. The boss lets his employees know where he stands; the leader lets his employees know where they stand. The boss uses people; the leader develops them.

I read a bit of graffiti this year on the side of an old building near my office: "People willing to roll up their sleeves seldom lose their shirt." Pitch in. Help out. Do more. You'll save a lot more than your shirt!

I was told once by a fellow employee that I'd be a better manager if I learned to intimidate. He suggested I read the book *Winning by Intimidation* and talked to me at length about the power that intimidation would produce for me.

I didn't follow his advice. I don't want power; I want respect. To me, intimidation creates fear and constant stress. And it most assuredly takes away a softness and kindness that I admire in a leader, be it a man or woman, Christian or non-Christian.

Clearly, it is important that we, as female professionals, be logical (a decision-making tool that is most frequently attributed to our male counterparts). But I think it is time that an equal amount of emphasis be placed on sensitivity, thoughtfulness, nurturing, and support so that the workplace is more comfortable, a place where each of us wants to spend our time and energy. And I firmly believe the result will be higher productivity!

Here are some suggestions for putting heart into your work:

(1) *When a job is well done, give a "perk"* —a thank-you note (with a copy to your supervisor), flowers, lunch, a couple of hours off early, etc.

(2) *Maintain an open-door policy,* inviting brainstorming and/or feedback on pertinent issues.

(3) *Don't be afraid to express your feelings as well as thoughts.* Encourage this in others.

(4) *Learn to love and enjoy the people with whom you work.* They are human beings as well as fellow employees. Inquire about their families, vacations, plans, dreams.

(5) *Be your unique self.* Don't duplicate someone else.

(6) *Don't always act your age.* Have fun on the job. Let some of the child in you show. Laugh.

(7) *Live out your aspirations.* Practice what you preach.

(8) *Don't be hard to get along with.*

This last suggestion reminds me of a comment made by Leontyne Price near the beginning of her opera career. She was featured on NBC-TV in a production of "Tosca," and after the production was completed she reminisced:

> Well, everyone involved at NBC has become a dear friend. And one thing that was most important is that I learned professionals really don't have to be difficult to get something accomplished. You could have a very relaxed atmosphere, and *mountains* are chopped down because everybody is so pleasant.[9]

That's it—chopping down mountains together in a relaxed atmosphere. That's professionalism with heart!

One's profession is a very personal thing. It cannot be inherited, nor can it be bequeathed. Only the person who puts to use her knowledge, courage, and heart with all her ability and complete dedication of purpose can truly be labeled a professional.

Notably present in a true professional are "quality of life" attributes—characteristics such as charm, tranquility, warmth, wisdom, peace, humor, and imagination. These are the issues of the heart. They make us beautiful, although they can't be put on with a powder puff nor removed with cleansing cream. The beauty of which they speak is achieved by living, loving, and learning.

Probably America's most beloved European actress is Sophia Loren. Born in a ward for unwed mothers in a small town near Naples, she was raised on a shoestring and sourbread in war-torn Italy. But her ultimate professional achievements and growth seem to have been enhanced by her meager, ignoble beginnings. Craving to find success and love, she defied every obstacle that stood in her way, learning all the while that dedication to purpose ultimately gets you where you want to go. Through the years she has only become more beautiful.

Asked to define her biggest beauty secret, Sophia Loren replied:

> It is only a "secret" because you never hear or read about it but I guarantee that it will make you more beautiful. It is a sense of inner peace. That is really my greatest beauty secret. People have often commented on this quality that I possess, but it is only recently that I have come to appreciate what they mean. I can't take credit for it. If I do have a sense of inner peace, it comes from my history, my experiences, my mother's strength, my personal faith, my children, so many things. And any tranquility I have is fragile. There are times when I am anything but tranquil . . . I have decided that tranquility is a great source of beauty, and so I am more aware of it than ever. Tranquility is a matter of being receptive—receptive to the small pleasures of life and to the satisfaction of goals achieved.[10]

Having a heart about our professional pursuits adds texture to our lives. It enhances relationships. It brings out the beauty of our inner souls. It sweetens our days of duties, making us more at peace and tranquil.

Element #4:
FAITH

The fourth and perhaps the most foundational ingredient which I feel is vital to becoming a Christian professional woman is faith. The Bible teaches that "faith is the substance of things hoped for, the evidence of things not seen."

Faith is different from courage. Courage involves stepping into the unknown with lots of questions: What's out there? Will I make it? Is it safe? Is it worth it? Do I dare? Questions about potential dangers, or difficulties. It's the idea of moving forward in fear and trembling—but moving.

Faith, on the other hand, involves stepping into the unknown with no questions. It is taking God at His Word. It is trusting because He is trustworthy. It is relying on Him because we are certain He will meet all our needs. It is confidence because He doesn't disappoint. Faith is moving forward without fear and trembling because we believe God will provide.

Faith always has an object, and the object of our Christian faith is the Lord Jesus Christ, the Son of God, who goes before us in every venture. Prayer is the link between us and God. We pray through Christ to God and we believe, without question, that God hears us and sets into motion the answer to our prayers. He may say yes, or no, or wait. But He does hear and answer.

All this must sound terribly simplistic to the reader who doesn't embrace the same belief. And it's impossible to explain fully because it can only be perceived in a supernatural way. But it works. For Christian professional women, our faith in Jesus can clarify direction on our course; it can lift us out of defeat into victorious living; it can provide company when we are lonely; it can literally work miracles.

I say "can" because, to make it work, we *must* believe it will. Belief sets faith into motion. Then, when faith moves, it's amazing how our bodies will follow suit.

Beverly Sills says, "Man plans, God laughs," and there's a lot of truth to that. We can do all the planning in the world, but God knows in advance where we're headed. Why not start out by asking Him first what He has in mind? Have the faith to believe that He will direct you on the proper and best pathway toward your professional niche. That's using your head!

Kaylan Pickford refers to faith as "the child in me." She claims that because children are rich in spirit and have a natural curiosity, they have ceaseless, spontaneous ideas which keep them darting from thought to thought, like bees from flower to flower. Faith should operate like that. Always reaching out. Always trying new things. Always looking forward to what God is going to do next. Faith is activated in direct proportion to our image of God and our belief in His ability to make a difference in our lives. With faith, nothing in the imagination is beyond reach. Anything can be played out or made to happen. Have the courage to act on your imaginations.

Sophia Loren expresses it this way, "It is easy to lose touch with the spiritual side of one's nature, and this is sad because it is a great source of peace and tranquility." When faith is active, there is solace.

Whatever you do, don't allow yourself to lose contact with God. Your relationship with Him is the cornerstone to your professional achievement. Believe that as you head toward your beautiful dream!

> There is ever a road that is winding
> With a signpost beckoning on;
> There is ever the glow of promise
> In the first golden rays of dawn.
>
> There is ever a friend that is waiting
> To guide and encourage with love.
> With cheer like the sunlight streaming
> Through our darkest sky above.
>
> There is ever a hope that is glowing
> And inspiring our efforts anew;
> Ever the goal that we cherish
> That gleams in the faraway blue.
>
> There is ever the prayer that is whispered
> For the joy tomorrow may bring;
> There is ever the faith to sustain us
> Till we find our beautiful dream.[11]

chapter three

The
Signposts

Thus in the beginning the world was so made that
certain signs come before certain events.

—CICERO
De Divinatione

ONE OF THE THRILLS of growing older is that life validates what we already know but have been unable to define. As frequently as we may have backtracked to find our way and felt we were starting over in the same old place, we were, in truth, not in the same place at all. At each juncture of "beginning again," we are a little wiser than before, and that modicum of wisdom, learned from experience, makes all the difference. With each step, we grow.

Growth does not come easily. There are peaks and valleys, good days and bad days. But all the while we are slowly moving ahead, changing for the better. That's what's important. As my brother Chuck says:

> Growing and learning are healthy, normal experiences. Both have to do with a process . . . and that process is sometimes painful, often slow, and occasionally downright awful! It's like taking three steps forward and two steps back.[1]

That third, unrepeated step is the one of victory that emerges out of the tough, incessant, daily struggle of trying to keep one step ahead of the hounds.

Rarely do we know with pristine clarity what we want to do with our lives at every given moment, because of the variables. And almost as rarely are we able to take stock of our progress, because we don't know where we are in the overall scheme of things. Are we in the middle of the journey, near the end, or still dillydallying somewhere around the starting gate? It is difficult to calculate progress without signposts. Therefore, I suggest we establish signposts on our professional journey that will both mark our way and advise us what to do next.

ANTICIPATE

As we have already discussed in chapter 2, true professionalism requires courage. A professional must have the conviction that her life is going in a particular direction toward a desired destination. To arrive there she must use her head *and* her heart, weaving a delicate web of work, caring, learning, risk, and faith in order to give her stability and purpose in the midst of this pursuit.

Now I'll go a step further. The professional woman must learn to anticipate her future—when to defer rewards, when to expect rewards, when to back off, when to move ahead, when to wait. She must develop a sense of timing.

If only there were flashing neon lights on our professional road warning us not to take the alternate route or that there was a bumpy road or trouble ahead. But we don't have that visual advantage. Therefore, to the degree that we are able, we must train our powers to anticipate what lies ahead so that we will know when to shift gears in advance.

What does the future mean to you? For many of us it means a time of reward. We work hard, make plans, put off immediate gratification in order to have something of value later on. To achieve future rewards, we must learn that everything cannot be had *now*. The richest life has a lot of waiting in it. And I don't mean "sit, soak, and sour" waiting. I mean present investment for future fulfillment. Working hard now to earn credentials later. Turning our dreams into reality by making use of present possibilities.

This is one of the reasons I value higher education. The time spent in study and preparation trains us for secondary reactions, not just immediate actions. By the simple discipline schooling requires, we learn to extend response time and delay gratification. Our diploma does not come at the end of today's work or tomorrow's tests, or even after the investment of one year. It is the outcome of years of endeavor. The educated individual is usually willing to postpone, to anticipate a better reward by having less now. This is very important, because the rewards that come over time are more bountiful than those received at the end of this hour or this week or this month.

Learning to anticipate also teaches us something a bit more subtle. The best choice does not always feel like the right choice, but by anticipating blessing in that decision we develop the strength of character to accept where we are, live through it, and go on. Three steps forward, two steps back.

A couple of years ago I took a "lifeline" test which was printed in *The Executive Female* magazine. It was a graph on which the participant was to draw a line representing her life from birth to her present age, showing major turning points such as jobs, marriage, divorce, schooling, successes, failures. The line slanted up and down as it ran from left to right, according to how well things were going at a given time. If the years or experiences weren't very good, the line sloped downward. If they were really bad—the pits—the line dipped very, very low. And the reverse was true for the good and very good years. The "so-so" years—not good, not bad, just average—ran in a straight line in the middle.

Interestingly, when I finished drawing the graph for my life, I noticed a revealing truth. First of all, very little of my life was on the average line. Most of it was above or far above. But there were two occasions, one in my early twenties and one in my early forties, where the line dipped very low.

The two lowest points in my life—I remember them well. The one in my twenties had to do with the pains of individuating, becoming my own person and discovering my own identity. The one in my forties was related to my acclimation to a new job and new surroundings where I felt there was no turning back. I experienced overwhelming regret for whatever decisions I had made that put me there.

In each case I felt trapped, unable to get out from under where I was. I experienced a loss of personal control and a gnawing torment in my spirit. I felt terrible all the time. I was in agony until my circumstances changed.

In looking back now, however, I realize that the most profound lessons I have learned about life were the byproducts of those two very low times. The circumstances didn't change until I got sick and tired of fighting myself, my ego, my dilemma, and God. I simply said to Him, "Okay, I'm fed up. Do what You will." Then He did. Almost immediately things got better. *Finally* He had gotten my attention and I had shut up.

Those occasions taught me that while life is capricious and unpredictable—often not what I want it to be—it is nevertheless within the scope of God's plan and purpose. What I thought was an absolute dead end was actually God's fertile proving ground. I hated it. But the principles I learned then I use every day in dealing both with myself and with other people. Those experiences demonstrated to me that no predicament is beyond God's light. My darkness is His opportunity to shine.

Notwithstanding these facts, not every reward need be deferred. Some of the sweetest rewards are for now, and we should anticipate them daily.

Although I knew the truth of Scripture and had experienced the presence of the Lord countless times prior to reading my "lifeline," when I saw the benefits in my human impasse, the realization of His unending provisions seemed to have renewed redemptive value. I was won again to His side. I was reminded of the loving nature of God—that He cannot make a mistake with my life. He promises me success and prosperity, courage, and strength as long as I obey

His Word. He commands me to tell other people these truths. When I do this, I can anticipate His presence on a moment-by-moment basis every day.

God speaks to us as He spoke to Joshua:

> Only be strong and very courageous; be careful to do according to all the law which Moses My servant commanded you; do not turn from it to the right or to the left, so that you may have success wherever you go. This book of the law shall not depart from your mouth, but you shall meditate on it day and night, so that you may be careful to do according to all that is written in it; for then you will make your way prosperous, and then you will have success. Have I not commanded you? Be strong and courageous! Do not tremble or be dismayed, for the Lord your God is with you wherever you go. (Josh. 1:7–9, NASV)

The promises of God and the power of His Spirit are mine to rely upon without ever waiting. No deferment. No postponement. They are a breath away, and for the problems that face the professional woman, that is great news. As one woman has said, "Don't be afraid of tomorrow; God is already there."[2]

> ## YIELD

We've all read Murphy's Laws—and, no doubt, we've seen many of them in action. There seems to be one to cover every conceivable situation. They're funny because they are so true.

For example, "If there are two events of importance, they will always conflict." Haven't you thought that on the night two of your favorite movies were being aired on television at the same time on different channels?

There are other old laws to live by that bear repeating:

Blake's Law:	The longer you save something for future possible use, the sooner you need it after it's destroyed.
Roe's Law:	No matter what happens, somebody knew it would.
Childer's Law:	When everything is perfectly clear to everyone, somebody didn't get the message.
Donsen's Law:	The specialist learns more and more about less and less until he knows everything about nothing.

Which brings me to Swindoll's Law—my own law—which I see in action almost daily:

Swindoll's Law:	Leaders who always have to do the job themselves usually do one on themselves.

Show me the leader who has never learned to delegate, and I'll show you the leader headed for burnout or an early grave. The fine art of delegation is one of the major keys to professional success, but many people would rather drown in a sea of paperwork, simply because they fear disaster: "If I don't do this myself, it won't be done right." And they wonder why their staff looks bored to death.

Delegation implies mutual commitment. Delegating responsibility says, "I trust you. You are an integral part of this organization. Your success is our success." Even though all the textbooks preach the virtues of delegation, rare is the manager, the supervisor, the professional, who delegates as a routine way of working.

There are many reasons for this:

- It will take longer to teach someone else to do it than to do it myself.
- This is so important it requires my personal attention.

- If I do it myself I minimize risk.
- What if I lose control of the job?
- What if she does a better job than I?
- What if there are errors?
- I might appear lazy if I give this to another person.
- Others will think I'm too close to my staff.

Sound familiar? Of course. Not only have we heard these reasons; if we've been in any kind of management position, we've said them ourselves.

But do you know from what source those words spring? From the empire builder. The empire builder always fears looking bad, losing control, risking repercussions. The woman who is building character, on the other hand, views delegation as an opportunity to teach and mentor as well as a practical measure to free her time for other areas needing attention. The paradox of delegation is, "The more often you delegate, the more committed you are to working with people. The more you give away, the more you take hold of your operation."[3]

One of the greatest gifts you, as a manager, can give those you manage is to teach them to become autonomous. Autonomous individuals function on their own evaluations, not yours. They don't feel manipulated. They are not peripheral, but integral in the network. Their feedback and brainstorming become unique and creative.

And mark my words—not one person above you will think you're lazy. On the contrary, your supervisors are going to be amazed at the team spirit, the high morale, and the enjoyable atmosphere that emanate from your department. You will see a level of production that you'd never know otherwise, because everybody will be working where the action is, as team players toward joint goals. It will be motivating. It will be contagious. And best of all, it will be fun. It all starts with yielding some of your authority.

I understand that not everything in the scope of your

responsibilities can be delegated. There are some things that only you can do—they have to do with your particular gifts, talents, training, or expertise.

When I am invited to speak, for instance, I cannot send a substitute. I am me, and I must represent myself. Similarly, when a professional lawyer or doctor or performer is hired to do a particular task, there can be no delegation.

But in cases like that, there's a second kind of yielding. When I accepted the challenge to write this book, there was no way for me to delegate that responsibility. The task was mine. This book was to be my thoughts, my philosophy about professional women, gleaned from my own life and experiences. Being accountable to my publisher for that commitment, and being unable to delegate any of the work, I then had to go to step two of yielding. I had to relegate the activities related to writing a manuscript to a certain order of action and accomplishment.

This book has been a long time in the making. I've done research, studies, interviews, questionnaires. I've written at times when I'd rather be playing. I've said no when I'd rather have said yes to certain invitations. I've put various other involvements on hold. I have set scores of "mini" deadlines to check project progress.

My motto: When you can't delegate, relegate! That is the only way in the world the busy person can accomplish many things. Even then, flexibility is the name of the game. We must be willing to yield in order to avoid possible collisions ahead.

CAUTION

Lily Tomlin said, "For fast-acting relief, try slowing down." No doubt, the most difficult question for the woman who is on the road to her professional niche is "When is enough, enough?" It is the haunting refrain that plays in our heads when we're not through with a project but we're dead tired; when we've been offered a better job with a bigger title and more money but the present position has nearly killed us; when one more sale, one more late night of work, one more trip out of town away from our family and friends will *surely* put us over the top. When is enough, enough?

It seems to be characteristic of high achievers to choose what is good for advancement but impoverishing to the spirit. We may be well rewarded, surrounded by possessions of quality, but find ourselves in a spiritual vacuum, with inner feelings of emptiness. Our acquisitions have been paid for by the loss of emotional and spiritual equilibrium. We simply want too much at the expense of our sanity.

In his fine book, *Modern Madness: The Emotional Fallout of Success,* Dr. Douglas LaBier writes,

> Passions for fame, power, and money, when they come to take over the person's reason for being and become ends in themselves, constitute forms of insanity.[4]

He points out that the most common consequence of this conflict of values is a feeling of self-betrayal. By embracing "careerism" with its perks and payoffs as a way of life, these "self-betrayers" have forfeited a life of meaning and integrity. They've given up something of themselves and now live with festering questions and self-criticism. He goes on:

> The new-breed careerist suffers emotionally when he or she makes decisions and choices which are bad, in the sense of limiting or distorting personal development and inner sense of meaning, although they seem attractive at the time because they are good for the career. Some poisons can taste good, but will still make you sick or kill you.[5]

What we're talking about here is balance, that wonderful stability we admire in others yet find so hard to achieve in ourselves.

65

The worrisome and somewhat surprising fact is that statistics show men are less likely than women to be married to their careers.[6] Somehow, we women see ourselves as forerunners to a new wave of female opportunities. We have to keep forging ahead to blaze the trail for the next generation of women. We're the pathfinders, the pioneers. So, without conscious realization, we seek to outdistance each other, damaging ourselves in the process.

It's all too easy to lose perspective. Therein lies a sinister, blinking danger signal. Typically, what happens is that the emphasis on competition produces such a strong desire to succeed that we sacrifice our sense of well-being for it. We work hard because we must, without time for other interests. Then later, when perhaps there is time to develop the balance, we find our careers are more rewarding than any other aspect of life, so we continue to lose ourselves in them. We never develop another life, nor do we stop long enough to tell ourselves, "This is enough!" And corporate structures are typically designed with policies that encourage such a loss of personhood for the benefit of achieving.

I worked with a woman like this once. Eager to prove herself worthy and ambitious to move ahead, she demonstrated a workaholism that surpasses any I've ever witnessed. She came early, stayed late, and on occasion even spent the night on a small sofa in the ladies' room so she could work as many hours as possible. She had no life apart from the office. The pity was that the more she worked, the less she seemed to catch up, much less get ahead. She became a frazzled, sleepless victim of a "modern madness" to achieve success. She betrayed herself and everything she wanted. Ultimately, because her work reflected more chaos and confusion than caring and control, she was fired—an embittered, tired, resentful woman.

This is an extreme case, I know. But wherever you are, if your whole life is work, you are walking into the same insidious psychological trap. It is so easy to get caught. Read the signposts along your professional road and take

66

heed. Remember, one's obsession with work doesn't come from the organization; it comes from one's self.

One of the sad, deceptive results of this type of ladder-climbing is that when we are in a management position, we begin demanding the same commitment from our employees. Because we made it to the top by working around the clock, we think others should do the same. Workaholics make rotten managers! There, I've said it.

Well then, where does the balance lie? How can I create private time for myself with such an impossible schedule? How can I replenish my spirit? How can I *know* when enough is enough?

Gail Sheehy, the author of *Passages* and *Pathfinders,* tells us:

> Would that there were an award for people who come to understand the concept of enough. Good enough. Successful enough. Thin enough. Rich enough. . . . When you have self-respect you have enough, and when you have enough, you have self-respect.[7]

Excellent—and oh, how true! Self-respect is the key to knowing when you have enough. It opens the door to personal satisfaction and a sense of fulfillment. When you love yourself and accept yourself for who you are, you have nothing left to prove.

With a little work, a little practice, and a lot of determination, you can develop the self-respect needed to pursue excellence. There's only one prerequisite, and it's major: *You must want it!*

Keep in mind that your balance and self-respect cannot be given to you by someone else. They are already inside you, waiting to be discovered and developed.

Look at it this way: Everyone is born with muscles, and everyone uses them. However, some people use them more than others. If you are willing to use your muscles—to exercise them with regularity and follow a sensible ongoing program for muscle development—you will become a healthier person, more in tune with your body. The same is true for the development of self-respect. Your willingness to commit yourself to shedding self-doubt in an ongoing program of development will make you a more assured, confident woman.

To reach this state of self-respect, try these ideas on a consistent basis:

(1) *Develop your own style* . . . in your grooming, tastes, furnishings, stationery, business cards, ideas. Become your *own* person, an original, not a copy of someone else. Be creative.

(2) *Work on your weaknesses.* When you spot shortcomings in yourself, don't be afraid to admit them. Apply elbow grease to bring about change.

(3) *Never give up.* What stands between mediocrity and excellence, between failure and success, are four words that lie within you: "I can do it!" Set your sights on your goal for self-improvement and keep working toward it. Do things. Be decisive.

(4) *Don't be afraid to ask questions.* We get where we're headed by inquiring about things we don't know. Ask questions. Make mental notes. Don't let not knowing intimidate you.

(5) *Admit when you are wrong.* Nobody's perfect, and nobody wants to be around someone who thinks he or she is. Ms. Perfect is a pain in the neck, so be vulnerable.

(6) *Develop hobbies and be actively involved in them* —reading, gardening, music, skiing, painting. There are thousands of enjoyable projects outside work that are waiting to be brought to life by you. Never lose your sense of wonder; let life be *wonder*ful.

(7) *Trust the gifts God has given you.* Each person is made uniquely. Use your talents without holding back, and bring them to bear on all of your experiences and decisions. You may discover gifts you never thought you had.

(8) *Be compassionate.* Thank other people for who they are and what they do. Show mercy and tolerance. Don't be

afraid to give your money for a worthy cause. Be generous in spirit and pocketbook.

(9) *Laugh a lot.* Don't take life and your situation too seriously or literally. Recognize that tomorrow's another day—that bad things don't last forever.

(10) *Daily commit your energies to the cause of Christ.* Say yes to the doors He opens. Spend time talking to Him, praising Him, thanking Him, and learning about Him. Walk by faith, believing He can and will bring you to maturity.

SLOW

The time comes in every professional journey when retirement has more appeal than the racetrack. Eventually it's time to slow down. For some of us this time is far in the future; for others just around the bend, but we would all do well to keep it in mind. As we negotiate this last leg of the road, there's no need to stop as long as our health remains, but there are reasons to rest more often, to reflect on where we've come from, to teach others about what to expect.

No matter where you are on the professional road, it's a good idea to get in touch with who you are now so that during your quieter years you can enjoy the companionship of yourself. At the same time, keep making new friends and enjoying new beginnings. Stop regretting endings. Life is full of change, crises, faded dreams—we know that by now. But those of us whose "life is hid with Christ in God" (Col. 3:1) will never run out of hope or the deepest kind of peace. Don't be afraid to sacrifice, remembering we can only keep what we give away.

Forgive yourself for the errors of the past and put them to rest once and for all. We've all made them. So what? Don't carry the weight of that guilt one more day. Dump it and leave it behind you. As my friend Lynda said in chapter 1, "leave that baggage on the road somewhere." Life is the process of discovering who we are and what we can accomplish. As we read the signposts and interpret them for ourselves, we understand where we are going. We learn what is possible and what is not.

Eugenia Zukerman, the professional flutist, leaves us with this thought:

> Learning is a procedure which evolves. If someone could give you that magic formula which would make you instantly a fine artist, you would be bored. Discovery is so important in your work, in relationships. In everything you do. It's the process that's important.[8]

And the process of discovery will continue to lead us from signpost to signpost on the road to our professional niche.

chapter four

The
Roadblocks

By now it should be clear that pathfinders are not magically shielded from surprise bumps in the road.

—GAIL SHEEHY
Pathfinders

SOMETIMES I'M DUMBER than I look. The truth of that disclosure was brought home to me recently on my way to work.

There are twenty-six miles of roadway from my home to my office. I drive that stretch daily, and I know it like the back of my hand. Most of it is freeway, but for the last four to six miles I have to thread my way through surface streets. During the past five months or so, those surface streets have been in a mess. The cities through which the streets pass are in the process of installing a massive underground sewer pipeline from point A to point B, and it seems to me that point A is just about where I leave the freeway and point B is somewhere beyond my office.

The streets are all torn up. There are trenches, metal plating, bumps, potholes, blinking warning signs, and traffic jams you wouldn't believe. All this confusion is intensified by gigantic pieces of equipment, with enormous tires and cranes and scoops and buckets, which come along and open the earth, fill it again with the concrete pipeline, compact it, and apply asphalt (seemingly done while I wait).

Needless to say, tempers flare. Horns honk. Rude gestures flash back and forth. One day some people behind me became so mad at the signalman, who was showing favoritism to a car full of guys he apparently knew, that they cursed at him and got out of the car grabbing handfuls of rocks to pelt him with when they got within throwing range. I was mesmerized by the scene, but unfortunately the light changed and I had to scramble ahead, leaving that scene of impending murder.

Like everyone else, I was sick of the whole mess: the roadblocks, the complications, the delay in getting to work. Every day I asked out loud in the car (just to hear my head rattle, since I drive alone), "Is this ever going to end?" My rattling head answered back, "Of course not, you fool. If it ever does you will have aged by then."

That became my daily diatribe: "Is this ever going to end?" Those six words ruled my morning from point A to B. I dreaded going to work because I hated those final few miles.

Well, one day I arrived at work out of sorts and mad at the world. I walked in—late, of course—and was mouthing my disgust with my unwelcome plight in life when one of the fellows I was talking with said, "Why don't you come to work a different way?"

"What do you mean, 'a different way'? There's only one way, and it's through that mess."

"No, Luci," he said. "Don't turn off 91 onto the surface street. Keep going until you meet up with the Harbor Freeway where 91 ends. There's a huge intersection there, and it's much less congested. I come that way every day."

"Hold it. You're trying to tell me there's no bottleneck at 91 and Harbor? You're crazy. I used to go that way, and it was such a mess I switched over to surface streets."

"Well, there hasn't been a bottleneck there for four or five months," my friend said. "Everybody must be going the way you are. Come the other way tomorrow and check it out yourself. Even if it's congested, it surely doesn't have all the roadblocks you've been running into."

Why I hadn't thought of that, I'll never know. The next day I switched, and the words "Is this ever going to end?" were replaced with "The smartest thing I ever did." Somehow, unwittingly, I had gotten in a rut, in a set way of doing something, feeling there was no way around it, hating it, griping about it, getting out of sorts over it, when finally someone called my attention to the fact that it didn't *have* to continue.

There was a way around those roadblocks. I just hadn't thought of it, as dumb as that may sound.

It's not always easy to act smart, to think smart, to be smart. We get in ruts—bogged down, blocked. And we stay there because we can't figure out how to get around whatever is keeping us from progressing.

The truth is, there are ways to maneuver around almost every roadblock in life—even if this means nothing more than changing our attitude toward the obstacle so that it's easier to cope with.

Besides, roadblocks are wonderful character builders. They help us grow up because they make us mad, and when we get mad enough with something that's blocking our way, we'll set about to change the situation.

My mother used to say, "We don't change until we get sick of ourselves." Development and growth often spring from those things in our lives or our circumstances which can no longer be tolerated. When we are blocked, we finally take action. We search for a way around or out of our "unwelcome plight." And sometimes we simply need a friend to suggest an alternate route.

For the woman who holds in her heart the dream of being a pro at what she does, it is impossible *not* to face roadblocks. This we need to know at the outset. At times roadblocks seem to appear out of nowhere. They are constructed by other people, or by society, or by tradition, history, the "norm," or stress. Sometimes we even build them ourselves!

The longer roadblocks are ignored or accommodated, the greater a problem they become. But we don't have to let this happen. Roadblocks are like bad habits which, when recognized and called by name, can be changed with the help of God and human determination. Just keep in mind when you come up against an irksome barrier, that they are designed to build character, not destroy it.

The problem is, we tend to want our troublesome situations changed *now*. We're sick of the obstacles and we want them out of the way immediately. But that's just not the way most problems are solved. More often, change comes by facing one day at a time.

Let's make that into a six-word slogan: *"Face one day at a time."* That is how *anything* is accomplished. There are no overnight cures. Before we can reach the niche we hope to attain, we must go on down the professional road, and going from point A to point B takes a great deal of strategy in getting over and around roadblocks.

In the all-black musical, *The Wiz,* which is a saucy, jumping take-off of that immortal fantasy, *The Wizard of Oz,* there is a song sung by Evillene (the Wicked Witch of the West) called, "Don't Nobody Bring Me No Bad News." It's terrific, and if you could plug earphones into this book and I could sing it to you now, I would, because it fits so well with what I'm saying.

Sometimes we get the blues over roadblocks. And not only the blues, but downright discouraged. We want to look at the world and say, "Don't nobody bring me no bad news. I can't take it. I'm sick of it. One more piece of it will do me in!"

But there *are* ways around; there *is* strength to go through "bad news." And one way is to do things minute by minute, one day at a time.

In my years of working in the corporate world, where I met and got to know executives and managers of all types, and in my fifteen years of professional singing with the Dallas Opera, where numerous stars and superstars crossed my path, I have had opportunity to observe a great many individuals. I have seen the ways in which a wide variety of professionals dealt with obstacles in their paths. I have also had some personal experience with roadblocks in my professional journey.

And what I have learned from all this is that most of the roadblocks I have faced in my career are the same ones faced by people of much greater influence and stature than I. Almost everybody comes up against these common barriers at some point in their career. So, out of the seedbed of my observation and experience, I'm here to tell you that roadblocks *can* be overcome. Let me suggest some ideas for getting around the most frequently encountered obstacles.

Roadblock #1:
FEAR OF FAILURE

The greatest roadblock of all in the life of almost every person I know is *fear of failure*. That's a dogmatic statement, but I believe it is true. This fear may take different forms, so it is sometimes difficult to recognize. But even the greatest men and women of history have had to struggle with feeling helpless and afraid, confused or infantile—or so historians later record. It is the rare leader who does not at some point in life become convinced that he or she has failed.

Most people like to excel. We want to do well, and we have a horror of failing. We prefer to please. As my brother says, we want to live above the level of mediocrity. The desire to achieve is ingrained in the human heart. People want to advance in their field of endeavor. This is right and good—may I say "normal"? I know of no one who wants to fail.

But interestingly enough, the fear of failure can manifest itself in widely varying kinds of behavior. Some people become paralyzed when decisions are called for because they fear any step they take will be the wrong one. Others seem to be driven forward by their fear. It sets in motion an impetus apart from their own drive or making, a sort of inner thrust. And it produces an almost supernatural power to achieve. Because this drive does not spring from a natural base of thinking, everything seems to get out of proportion.

For example, someone might take a promotion that is justifiably offered, but be scared to death she will be found in time to be an impostor—undeserving of the honor and responsibility. Or the Peter Principle may come into play and she will accept a position for which she is truly not qualified, but feels she must accept because declining is an indication of failure. Then all she can do is tread water as fast as possible, hoping she won't be discovered. In either case, the going is rough and the anguish is real.

In 1985 Pauline Clance, a psychologist at Georgia State University, wrote an interesting book entitled, *The Impostor Phenomenon: Overcoming the Fear That Haunts Your Success.* She points out that successful people who suffer from fear of failure often encounter a strange paradox—they keep succeeding. These are people who never feel their success is genuine. Consequently, they always feel the pressing need to prove themselves once again.

This feeling is the opposite of low self-esteem. The person with low self-esteem feels unworthy or inadequate to the task—and will usually "freeze up" from fear of failure. But the successful "impostor" keeps on moving right up to the finish line—feeling all the while that she is "faking it." These people know they're successful, but they also "know" they have gotten where they are only through luck or charm. So they keep redefining success. "When they get a success, they raise the definition of real success another rung on the ladder," Clance says. "If they've done one good movie, next time they need to do a bigger, better movie. And the next time, if they don't win an Oscar, it's obvious to themselves that they're just fakes after all."[1]

Fear of failure drives us into very interesting alternate routes, doesn't it? Danuta Soderman, the cohost to "The 700 Club," probably the most widely watched program in Christian television, tells of how she overcame this malady. At the age of seventeen, she confesses, she was extremely shy. Living in Alaska with her mother after her parents' tragic divorce, she became deeply confused and had no confidence in herself. Being certain that she would never amount to anything in life, she was completely down on herself.

Her mother found an ad in the newspaper for the Miss Anchorage Beauty Pageant. She asked Danuta, "Why don't you enter this?"

Danuta said, "I can't do that! I can't stand up there in front of everybody and act like I'm perfect. People will look at me, and they'll know I'm not perfect."

Her mother replied, "All you have to do is walk on that stage and act like you own the joint. And nobody will know that you don't."[2]

Those six words, *"Act like you own the joint,"* made a lasting impression on Danuta Soderman. She entered the contest, and every time she got scared she remembered that line. She not only won the talent division, but also got second runner-up in the contest. She says that from the moment she knew that other people saw value in her, she began to feel that maybe she had value. "Waking up to that was the beginning of the beginning for me," she said.

Oh my! The times I have feared failure—I've lost count. I recall several years ago when I became a manager with Mobil Oil Corporation's West Coast Pipelines Department. I was scared to death. Offered the promotion, I vacillated between accepting and rejecting it. Can I do it? What if I don't know enough? I'm not qualified. I'm apt to make mistakes. On and on my reasoning went, filling me with self-questioning and self-doubts. This was a bigger job than I had ever held in my life, with greater responsibilities and greater chances for bombing on a massive scale.

I remember talking with a close friend of mine in the Dallas Mobil office at that time. Her name is Martha Daniel. She is retired now, but then she was serving as a coordinator in the Employee Relations Department and personally knew many executives in the corporation. I voiced my fears and concerns to Martha, not really expecting that her input would be of the value to me that it was. More than anything, I think I was seeking sanctuary for my troubled spirit.

Martha listened carefully to all my misgivings and woes, then she said something which I firmly believe was the deciding factor in my accepting the offer.

"Of course you can do the job, Luci. No question about it. You'll be perfect for it," she said. "Just remember two things: Never sign anything until you're sure, and don't be afraid to ask questions. Everybody on the management level asks questions. That's how things are learned."

Not a single day passes in my career that I don't think about and use Martha's expert advice. Although given off the cuff, it has helped me immensely. In the same way, "Act like you own the joint," was given with little thought, but it changed a woman's life.

We *need* to hear remarks like that from people we respect, we need to pass them on to others, and we need to remind ourselves of them. *Everybody* is faking it—or thinks she is. Some of us are a little more vulnerable than others, but that's okay. We're stepping out there on faith, moving toward a worthy goal, taking a risk. Trying something—anything—is clearly better than smothering in fear of failure.

At the same time, if we are among those successful "impostors" who push *because* they fear failure, we will never have a place to stop and rest. The cycle will exhaust us because, in order to feel good about ourselves and our profession, we must do more and more and more. And the result will be professional burnout.

Early in our professional pursuit, we must learn there is a limit to how much one can sacrifice in pursuit of advancement. Our bodies have natural limits, and we need to heed the rhythm of our bodies to know when to slow down or absolutely stop.

You know what professional burnout says to me? It says the individual who suffers from it is still an amateur, not a professional. It says she took off from the starting gate fueled by bravado, enthusiasm, and expectation, but didn't consider the real cost.

An amateur doesn't look ahead. She lives for the first few blocks, not the whole race. And you know what? If she changes jobs the story will be the same, because burnout doesn't come from the occupation, it comes from the person who has never ordered her priorities or exercised basic management skills. She may have an executive title, priding herself on accomplishing her job and everyone else's, hanging around her place of business for eighteen hours a day, calling all of this "initiative," but she's never learned to delegate, defer rewards, relegate—in short, use her head.

When burnout occurs, the very best thing one can do is pull over to the side and evaluate. Recognize what was done that caused burnout in the first place. Back off. Let go of the high-powered control reins. Get out into the real world and start developing a private life, with family, friends, church, sports, activities. The burned-out woman needs to realize her professional sights were set too low, not too high. When she thought she had arrived, she was actually only beginning. Burnout teaches that lesson—the hard way.

Roadblock #2:
PROCRASTINATION

Another roadblock that impedes progress almost as much as fear of failure is *procrastination*. The procrastinator has never learned to tell time. It's that basic. Even though procrastinators are preoccupied with time, it remains an enigma to them—as odd as that may sound. They are constantly assessing how much they have left to do and how little time they have to do it in, instead of using that time to get it done.

Procrastinators are interesting people, often very charming, because they operate their lives and talk in the realm of potentials and possibilities, in a fantasy world of fun and games. They are wishful thinkers, always hoping to find more time than there is on the face of a clock or from dawn to sunset.

The very fact that time is exact, fixed, measurable, and finite is difficult, almost impossible for the procrastinator to accept. Then, when they are caught short, they are actually surprised or, worse, offended at the clock, themselves, or whoever is at hand upon whom they can lay blame.

What makes people procrastinators? Many things. Some don't quite know how to handle a task, so they put it off. Some people feel overwhelmed or dislike what has to be done. Others operate under the eleventh-hour syndrome because it gives them a "high." The adrenaline pumps and the mind races, and this adds excitement to an otherwise boring routine. (I have friends who seem to do their best work during the eleventh hour, but for me it would be disaster. I'd feel I was sitting on a powder keg.)

As I said, procrastinators are charming people. But when this habit affects one's work or professional status, it becomes a luxury that cannot be indulged. It blocks one's way to achievement and success.

There has been a lot of information written on procrastination, how to manage one's time, how to get up and get going. Much that is written is excellent and worth applying in our daily lives. I try to use what I have learned and am learning because I, too, am occasionally plagued with voluntary inertia, although I dislike that in myself and fight it tooth and nail.

There are four principles I apply to help me detour around this all-too-common roadblock. Maybe they'll be of benefit to you as you try to do them in this order:

(1) *Identify the types of procrastination situations.* What rings your procrastination bell? An unpleasant task? An overwhelming or complex project? End results being too far away? Solitude? Being afraid of what the results will be?

Fear of failure? Feeling stymied? Mercy! It can be practically anything. Name it for what it is and write it down.

(2) *Divide the task into manageable parts.* Here is probably the best principle the procrastinator can learn. Nothing of value is accomplished overnight. Remember that! Everything is a process, and processes take time. Little minutes here and there, put together, create the whole:

Losing weight. Building a house. Writing a book. Mastering a sport. Saving money. Getting an education. Rearing children. Learning a language. Whatever it is, start early and work a bit at a time. If need be, chart your course and your progress on paper, but never give up. I didn't say, "never stop," or "never have fun," or "never take a break." I said "never give up."

If you fear going to the doctor, for instance, because you anticipate what he'll tell you, start by looking up his number and writing it down. Then have a cup of tea and a time of prayer with the Lord. Tell Him of your fear and anxiety. Ask for His peace and courage. When your prayer is over and your teacup empty, put your hand on the phone and make that call. Stay calm. Keep remembering you've asked for God's courage. Use it! State your message and ask for an appointment. Prepare daily for that appointment by doing what you can physically, mentally, and spiritually.

When the appointment time comes, go. Try to relax. Call to mind the Scripture you've memorized and believe it! Receive what the doctor tells you like a grown-up, like the professional person that you are, and act accordingly.

Maybe the news won't be nearly as bad as you feared. Maybe it will be worse. But at least you'll know, and your procrastination—on that score anyway—will be over.

Whatever the task that faces you, start at the beginning and systematically move toward completion. I promise you will complete whatever it is if you once start and keep moving forward in manageable sections.

(3) *Don't ever wait to be prodded.* You have a novel idea you think will work? State it. Express yourself.

Several years ago, I read *Blackberry Winter*, the autobiography of Dr. Margaret Mead. Repeatedly, I was intrigued by this unique woman whose new ideas literally forged out pioneering achievements in the world of anthropology.

Dr. Mead's father once said to her, "It's a pity you aren't a boy; you'd have gone far." But how much farther could she have gone? This woman, who never waited to be prodded, liberated herself from convention, living life to the full. She was crowned with awards and medals and honors because she dared unprecedented feats of adventure and saw them to completion, changing the course of anthropological findings forever.

Admittedly, most of us operate on a much smaller scale, but it's the same principle. Don't allow discrimination or tradition to hold you back. We live in a world chock-full of challenges for women. If some challenging undertaking is on the tip of your professional dream, don't wait to be prodded. Take the first step and turn a deaf ear to the wooing of procrastination.

(4) *Save some prime time for yourself.* Something I learned a long time ago is that I do a lousy job on my hair. Yes, my hair. I'm not adept at that necessary function of good grooming. On the days I was to wash my hair, I found I dreaded it all day or all night, whichever the case was, because I knew when I was finished it still wouldn't please me, no matter how hard I tried. That very dread pulled my spirit down. Every other day I was low because of this silly, impending obligation I could not manage well.

Then one day it hit me: "Luci, pay to have your hair done. It's worth it to the balance of your spirit, not to mention those who have to look at you."

So I did. In fact, I now have my hair done twice a week at a local beauty shop where I know everybody, and we have lots of fun chatting and swapping stories. Even though Anni is my usual operator, every operator in that shop has done my hair at some time or another. I am the regular of all regulars, and I love it.

What is it in your life that pulls your spirit down or makes you dread getting up in the morning or coming home at night? Fix it! If your house never suits you because it's out of order, and you have no time or inclination to do it yourself, pay to have a housekeeper or cleaning person. You'll be amazed how that simple choice of delegation can free your mind and lift your spirit, enabling you to live in surroundings that are straight and clean, apart from your doing.

If you don't enjoy cooking, eat more meals out. You don't have to go to the Ritz. Find a nice neighborhood restaurant that's not too expensive and give yourself that luxury. Have your necessary typing done. Get a babysitter for the kids two nights a week. I know of women who even have a paid clothes consultant at their beck and call.

The point is, with all you have to do as a busy professional, if you have a tendency to procrastinate because of overwhelming duties that are unrelated to work, delegate some of that, too. The change in your spirit will amaze you. It will cost you a bit of money, and you may have to juggle your budget boundaries, but take it from one who has the hairdo to prove it—it's worth every penny to give you more prime time for yourself. Many of the things you dread in your private life will take a back seat in your hierarchy of duties and anxieties. That's very important to your mental health.

For those of you who are procrastinators and have no desire to change, may I suggest you consider joining the Procrastinators Club of America. Their motto is, "Time is too valuable to fritter away on the essential." The founder, a Philadelphian named Les Waas, originated the club on a whim in 1956 when he and co-workers joked about "scheduling a meeting just for the sole purpose of postponing it." They advertised the never-to-be meeting, drew some responses, and repeatedly canceled it. In 1984 the membership had grown to 4,400, with Waas speculating that half a million people would be joining as soon as they got around to it. Official members receive a membership card, a License to Procrastinate (ideal for framing), a pin, bumper stickers, and a copy of last month's newsletter. Mr. Waas suggests that those who want to join write for information whenever they find the time: Procrastinators Club of America, 1111 Broad-Locust Building, Philadelphia, PA 19102. As I said, there are all sorts of ways to maneuver around roadblocks. . . .

Roadblock #3:
TRANSITION

The third roadblock that clutters the route toward our professional niche is *transition* . . . change, and all that goes with it.

Over the past thirty years or so, a number of studies have been conducted related to the effects of change in a person's life. Evidence suggests that too many changes—whether controllable or uncontrollable, positive or negative—can actually make a person sick. To measure this, certain events have been assigned numerical values and are referred to as "life-change units." Such events as marriage, changing jobs, losing a job, death of a loved one, birth of a child, excessive debts, divorce, jail terms, moving to a new location, and so on, can be measured in terms of "life-change units." The greater the number of these units in a person's life at a particular time, the higher the risk for illness.

What can we do about that? Changes take their toll to different degrees on different people. Some bounce back effectively or even thrive on change, while others fall apart. Why? It seems that those who cope best with change are the persons with resiliency—the ability to adapt to the after-effects of change. In other words, they are the persons who learn to fight change with change—they beat it at its own game, so to speak. The answer lies in *learning to adjust one's expectation levels* through planning.

What does this mean in practical terms?

If you are planning to move, start getting ready months in advance. Talk with people who have moved; write down the details of what they tell you so you can look at them and reflect on them. Be in prayer about your move; ask the Lord to begin the adjustment in your mind and heart immediately. If possible, visit your new home or city. Practice thinking about the positive aspects of the move. Don't dwell on the negatives; commit those to God.

What you are doing is getting rid of a lot of the unknowns first. And the reason change can be such a roadblock is that we are going into the unknown, and the unknown is often deeply debilitating.

If you are having surgery, become familiar with what is going to happen. You'll heal faster if you understand more. If you're going to a new job in a company, ask those who have been there what it's like. Read books and articles about people who have served in similar capacities. Expect reality. Instead of imagining the best or the worst prospects, choose the middle. There are trade-offs in everything, and we need to adjust our thinking to accommodate those trade-offs. Unknowns intimidate; therefore, know all you can up front.

Sometimes, during transition times, it simply helps to focus more intently on your goals. Goals minimize the effects of change because they make us impervious to side effects, and to the goal setter, change is nothing more than a negative side effect. The dream is out there in the distance. Focusing on it makes us less aware of and less bothered by the changes that are occurring closer to home. We see the dream on the horizon, not the change over by the side of the road.

Change may be a source of irritation, but as Barbra Streisand sings, it won't "rain on our parade." Stand back and view your life objectively from time to time, trying very hard not to blow situations out of proportion. Simply because you are experiencing a life-change unit this month or this year doesn't mean you will experience it every year until the day you die. God designs these things at certain times in our lives for His own purposes.

One of the signs of a truly Christ-centered professional is the maturity to distinguish between that which is going to pass and that which is going to last. There are occasions when we must maintain, continue, endure, no matter how much we are criticized, discriminated against, or buffeted. A lot of life is maintenance work, keeping our spirits vulnerable to God's shaping and honing. Not giving up. Not caving in.

It is our responsibility to learn continuity. But our continuity is tied to a relationship with Christ, not a relationship with this world. By our commitment to Him and His calling for our lives, He enables us to transcend that which would otherwise make us sick, sap our strength, or take away the joy of life.

As Christians we, at times, have the mistaken idea that once we put our life into God's hands, everything is going to be predictable, stable, and permanent. This reasoning leads us into the delusion that troubles should not come our way.

Then when transitions and problems occur, taking their toll on our spirits and bodies, we wonder what happened, and we often fall apart. We tire of the struggle and our own human frailties. We no longer want to "run with endurance the race that is set before us" (Heb. 12:1, NASV). We're sick of the whole mess and want to throw in the towel, because we are looking for and expecting certainty, *not* change.

But in this life, certainty is a myth! Here's what we need to remember—these encouraging, wonderful words from Dr. Daniel Taylor:

> We do not choose between a life of difficulty and a life of ease. We simply choose *for what purpose* we will work,

sometimes suffer, and hopefully endure. I may have more pain than my secular neighbor; I may have less. In either case, my struggles are given an ultimate meaning by the context of a life lived in light of eternity.[3]

That's the key to dealing with change: *always look for an ultimate meaning!* Christian working women, please hear this once again: God is in the business of building our characters, not our empires. Therein lies *His* purpose for working on us and *our* purpose for working on ourselves, and therein lies the reason for transition.

God offers us a person and a relationship; we want rules and a format. He offers us security through risk; we want safety through certainty. He offers us unity and community; we want unanimity and institutions. And it does no good to point fingers because none of us desires too much light. All of us want God to behave Himself in our lives, to touch this area but leave that one alone, to empower us here but let us run things ourselves over there.[4]

This issue of transition is particularly applicable to a large and growing group of women in the professional ranks: working mothers.

With the opening up of new opportunities for women in the work force and the resulting exodus from the home, there has developed an unfortunate division among women, almost a cold war. And the subject of the war is motherhood.

Too often, the traditional mother who believes her place is in the home, rearing her children and finding her means of significance in total integration with family— their routines, problems, and hopes—harbors animosity toward the mother who chooses to work outside the home. The woman who has a career, on the other hand, harbors these same feelings of enmity toward her conventional counterpart.

Who makes the better mother? Battle lines are clearly

drawn, and whichever side the mother chooses, she can expect to be criticized and experience reverberations. There are national organizations supporting both views and extremely strong feelings of loyalty in both camps.

Let me say at the outset that I am not a working mother. I am a single, childless, working professional who has observed this war from the sidelines and simply formed opinions. That's all. I do not pretend to be an advocate of either point of view, and the only reason I raise the issue here is that both groups of women are facing on a daily basis a unique transition and dilemma that should be acknowledged.

This transition is cultural, with no antecedents for guidance. Women do not have the history behind them to know the long-term implications of their choices.

If the traditional mother chooses to stay at home, feeling this is her duty before God, she often has the discomforting thought that had she chosen a profession she might have been a richer person in spirit, a better mother, a more integrated individual into the whole of society. She views her life as being deficient.

By the same token, the mother who reports to the workplace outside her home fights the fear that she is not the mother she should be. Life seems to fall into jagged pieces, fragmented and disquieting because of her varied purposes. She views *her* life as being deficient.

Each lifestyle leads to ambivalence about one's own choices. As if these forces of turmoil within were not enough, there is the battle between the two groups of women without. And to resolve the conflict, each mother feels she must justify the correctness of her choice and somehow irrefutably prove this to the opposing side.

No mother has ever verbalized the battle internally and externally better than Prime Minister Golda Meir, mother of two children herself, who also ultimately came to be known as the mother of modern Israel:

There are mothers who work only when they are forced to. . . . But there is a type of woman who cannot remain home for other reasons. In spite of the place which her children and her family take up in her life, her nature and being demands something more; she cannot divorce herself from a larger social life. She cannot let her children narrow her horizon. And for such a woman, there is no rest. . . . this eternal inner division, this double pull, this alternating feeling of unfulfilled duty—today toward her family, the next day toward her work—this is the burden of the working mother.[5]

Research shows that a woman's satisfaction with her role in life makes all the difference in how good she is at parenting, even though she may suffer from frequent inner conflicts. It boils down to how the individual mother feels about herself as a person.

Obviously, Golda Meir had a calling to provide social guidance for a nation, something most mothers do not face. At the outset of her marriage at a young age, she told her husband, Morris, of her dream that Jews must have a land of their own and that she must help to shape it. Reluctantly, he agreed to go to Palestine and live in a kibbutz. He hated it. Morris wanted his wife for himself, and refused to have children unless they left the kibbutz.

Golda acquiesced. They moved to a tiny apartment in Jerusalem, where their son was born. But she still felt the pull to play a role in the life of the nation, and she felt like a prisoner in her own home. Naturally, she hated that.

After the birth of a second child, and the bitter resentment that rose in her heart at being prevented from doing the work in Palestine to which she felt she was called, Golda accepted the defeat of her marriage and returned to work in the movement. She was criticized for being "a public person, not a homebody." Her mother chastised her, as did her sister, the revolutionary who had ignited Golda with the Zionist dream in the first place. Even with all the fine work she accomplished for her country, she suffered from guilt that taunted her to the end of her life for not having been a "model mother."

The reason that I used this story is that it conveys the ongoing dilemma: Are working mothers "good" mothers? The fact is this can never be solved by a pat answer that applies to everyone. It *can't* be solved because it is a subjective and relative question. *Who* can judge? The Nation? The mother's relatives? Or . . . the mother herself? If the story left this question in your mind "Was Golda as good a mother as she was a national leader?" then I have accomplished my purpose. This feeling is exactly what every working mother faces on a smaller scale. And I believe it is okay not to have an answer.

After all, who is the model mother? What does that entail? I know mothers who stay at home for the good of the family as well as themselves, and mothers who work outside the home for exactly the same reason. Yet, there are times when they both wind up doing laundry and grocery shopping in the middle of the night—not because that's motherhood, but because that's life. As an unmarried woman, without children, I do that, too, and it can't be helped. We are each called to many responsibilities that must be carried out, and to accomplish these responsibilities, *realize your composure lies in balance.*

Good mothers come in all types. The more contented you are with the overall character being built in your life, the better parent you will be, and the better professional woman you will become. My plea is that the war of the employed versus the nonemployed mother be ended in a truce. Accept each other as allies instead of adversaries, and work together to bring about the changes that will enhance the cause of Christ. Stop quibbling about the arena in which you spend the majority of your time. We have much bigger battles to fight as Christian women.

Roadblock #4:
POOR COMMUNICATION

The final roadblock I want us to consider is *poor communication*. How we communicate as professional women can make us or break us.

In my mind, successful communication requires two elements that many in the working world neglect: knowing how to talk and knowing how to listen. Sounds simple enough, doesn't it, but it's more difficult than it sounds. In a sense, there's an art to it. Generally, people love to exchange light, easy conversation. They like to laugh and joke and feel relaxed. It has been my experience that employees or colleagues respond more readily and favorably to a supervisor or leader who can make small talk with them. Lee Iacocca, bestselling author and Chief Executive Officer of Chrysler Corporation, puts it so well, "You don't succeed for very long by kicking people around. You've got to know how to talk to them, plain and simple."[6]

That's the secret: plain and simple. Breaking the ice! It can seem, on occasion, like a waste of time, yet it has the power to open doors to serious discussions and vital brainstorming.

Dr. Georgette McGregor, who was a professor of speech before she became a full-time consultant and communications expert says, "I noticed when I began to work with people who were skilled at big talk that it was something they'd learned how to do. But they really didn't feel at ease with small talk."[7] She points out that while these individuals were successful scientists, specialists, leaders in big corporations, they generally were not successful at communicating with co-workers and employees.

Casual conversation reflects that you yourself are relaxed and confident about who you are and where you are. You're not standing there wondering what others are thinking of you; you're enjoying what's going on. Small talk is a nonthreatening meeting ground that is effective in leading to deeper exchange of creative ideas, thoughts, and feedback.

Here's our six-word key to managing small talk: *Focus in on the other person.* Ask questions. Exhibit genuine interest. Be informal, without a "let's get down to business" attitude. Show that you care about other people as persons, not objects. Once you've done this, it's amazing how much easier it is to get down to business.

In her excellent book, *Choosing the Amusing,* my dear friend Marilyn Meberg writes:

> At work we may spend years with our fellow employees, seeing in them only their success or failures and knowing nothing of their inner life because they are merely objects to us. When they succeed and that success enhances our work environment, we are pleased they have functioned well. When they fail, and that failure inconveniences us, we are irritated.[8]

Right on, Marilyn! That's so true. Too true, unfortunately. But there's hope:

> There have been many times when someone ceased to be an object of irritation to me once I heard his or her heart, listened to his or her insecurities, and watched the protective mask slowly lower as I revealed my own insecurities. When I heard that heartbeat in such close synchronization with my own, the person ceased to be an object. That would never have occurred without time and concentration upon our respective persons. Such a focus caused me to understand as well as empathize with what had formerly irritated me. As a result, the person ceased being a performing object and became a valuable person.[9]

That's a long quote, but the principles Marilyn states are foundationally important to the Christian professional woman. Interested in the development of character in both herself and others, she *must* care about people as persons. Or, as Dr. McGregor states it, she must be "eternally fascinated." Don't miss that double meaning.

In October 1986, *Working Woman* magazine printed a list of the twelve key ingredients of a satisfying job. Listed in the order of their importance, number one was "Interesting and challenging work," and number two was "Management that makes employees feel they are important as individuals."

I am not saying constructive criticism doesn't have a place, but I *strongly* feel that negative appraisals of employees would be minimized if supervisors simply chatted with people "plain and simple" rather than knocking them dead with a list of their faults. Managers are called to nurture and build, not condemn and destroy. It begins with learning how to chat.

Our last six-word slogan deals with the other side of the communication coin: *try to become an attentive listener*. I have to refer again to *Choosing the Amusing* because knowing from experience what a superb listener Marilyn is, I can testify that the three suggestions she gives us to be attentive ("empathic," she calls it), really work:

- Listen with your whole body.
- Don't interrupt.
- Enter into the mind and the emotion of the person speaking.[10]

Marilyn encourages us to listen empathetically to others, advising us that this kind of listening mends the spirit as well as lifts the heavy heart.

You're saying, "I don't have time for that stuff. I've got deadlines. I've got a show to run. I don't have the luxury of taking time to zero in on other people, listening and chatting."

But hear me carefully: I'm not advocating you shut down the shop while everybody sits around all day cracking jokes, drinking coffee, and chatting. I'm advocating that you *care* . . . you care enough to show sympathy, sensitivity, and—dare I say it again—vulnerability.

Believe me, one of the lovely things about being a feminine professional is that you need not denigrate what comes naturally to you by virtue of being a woman. "What business needs is what women know how to do."[11]

When leadership studies were conducted with the first coed classes at West Point, traditionally a stronghold of masculine values, an interesting fact emerged. While males and females scored equally well on "getting the job done," in the evaluations by their subordinates, women were rated higher when it came to looking out for subordinates' welfare and showing interest in their lives. Networking and teamwork should be second nature to us women. Most of us are used to "picking up signals" about people. As we learn to positively respond to those signals, we not only build communication skills, we build our character. And that's what true professionalism is all about.

Reflect with me a minute: fear of failure, procrastination, transition, poor communication. Are you unable to get from point A to point B because of one of these roadblocks? Try these detours:

- Face one day at a time.
- Act like you own the joint.
- Identify the types of procrastination situations.
- Divide the task into manageable parts.
- Don't ever wait to be prodded.
- Save some prime time for yourself.
- Learn to adjust your expectation levels.
- Always look for an ultimate meaning.
- Realize your composure lies in balance.

- Focus in on the other person.
- Try to become an attentive listener.

No more delays. No more potholes or barricades. No more construction equipment blocking your path. No more being out of sorts. You've discovered an alternate route—so start your engine and get moving!

chapter five

Fellow
Travelers

As women try out new roles and take greater, more visible risks, many are discovering the importance of sharing their experiences with others who have similar concerns. . . . Obviously this kind of cooperation and support doesn't just happen. It takes time, care, and commitment to build a network that really works.

—MARILYN LODEN
Feminine Leadership

IF YOU'RE LIKE ME, you're fascinated by people. They never cease to be interesting—their fads and fashions, quirks and foibles, hopes and dreams.

I enjoy reading biographies because I like to know what others are like inside—how they think and face problems, and what they do to come through them. And I like biographies with pictures because I want to see how people look. As the story unfolds, I like to flip over to the photographs and see, once again, the individual to whom all this is happening—to get a feel for that person's character. It helps me to know that the subjects of biographies look normal—two eyes, a nose, a mouth. They're "one of us." A photograph gives me a visible image with which to identify.

Not only do I enjoy reading about heroes and heroines whose accomplishments are so outstanding they leave us breathless; I also like to read about "hometown heroes." These are people who live in our neighborhood, go to and from work, deal with joys and sorrows like the rest of us—in short, people who live ordinary lives. But these hometown heroes have something extra: the ability to live an ordinary life in an extraordinary way. The secret lies in their attitude about life. Their faith. Their courage. Their purpose.

In this chapter I would like to introduce you to five women who are "hometown heroes" of mine when it comes to the career journey. They come from different backgrounds and their careers have taken them down very different paths, but each in my mind embodies the kind of true professionalism this book is all about. They are the women to whom this book is dedicated—and this chapter consists of their stories.

I interviewed each one of these friends with some specific questions in mind. I was interested in the road they took to achieve their niche and what they encountered along the way. I also wanted to know their ideas about professionalism and their attitudes toward their careers. I was looking both for the qualities these women had in common and the things that made them different. And I specifically wanted to know how their Christian faith had affected their careers.

Each one of the women you'll meet in this chapter was initially very reluctant to be called out and featured in an interview. Although honored, none of them felt "worthy." They were gracious because that's their nature, but each one said, "Are you sure you want me, Luci? I mean, I haven't done anything special. What can I say that will benefit others? I'm just me."

But that's just the point! The world is made up of "just mes"! Just ordinary folks, energized by God's Spirit to do things extraordinarily. That's exactly why I chose these women. They're like us. Their gifts or talents may differ from yours or mine—they may be taller or shorter, older or younger. But under the skin, on the gut level, they feel and hope and strive and hurt and desire and dream like you and me.

As you read the following interviews, I hope you recognize that these women, who have accomplished so much, have the same fears and needs you have. As you look at their pictures, I hope you can tell they're normal folks—two eyes, a nose, a mouth, just like you. I hope their accomplishments show you how much is possible when women trust God and keep moving ahead in spite of obstacles, both internal and external. And I hope you find yourself saying, "If they can do it, I can do it too!"

There's something else I hope you pick up from this chapter—an understanding of why it is important to have a network, or support system, on the professional journey.

The women who are featured in this chapter, among others, are my network. If you haven't discovered it already, you're going to find as a career woman that such a group of supportive friends and colleagues is one of your most important assets—it is vital to your emotional, mental, and spiritual health.

Through the years these women and I have kept in close touch, sharing joys and sorrows. We have listened to each other's frustrations about "the system"—whichever system we were encountering at the moment! We've exchanged ideas and information. We've wept together. Prayed together. Laughed together. Vacationed together. These connections and relationships are imperative to my professional life.

The purpose of networking is not necessarily to solve or transcend problems—sometimes that's just not possible. Instead, a network is for brainstorming, encouraging, listening, lifting, laughing, sharing mutual frustrations, and providing sanctuary on a level of common bonding. Frequently, those in my network have come to one another crippled or hurting, looking for a crutch or solace, and we have found the wonderful, healing touch we needed.

These friends, all professional women, have never sought to control my behavior or to force me into being something I'm not. They have loved me and encouraged me on my own path. More often than they know, their affirmation has kept me going when I really wanted to quit. For that, I offer them my sincere thanks.

But now, you must get to know them too:

Traveler #1:
MARLENE KLOTZ
(b. October 28, 1950)

MUCH LIKE BEVERLY SILLS, who began singing at the age of three, my friend Marlene demonstrated very early that she had an innate sense of her ultimate niche. Even at age five, she enjoyed helping others, exhibiting interest in their growth and development. Each afternoon she would gather up a small band of "students" and impart to them what she herself had learned to read that day. One afternoon she emerged from the bedroom clutching her head in her hands and reported to her mother, "These kids will never learn!"

In high school, Marlene was responsible for organizing the clothing drive for "Save The Children," active in student government, and intensely involved in the area of journalism. "I've always loved reaching out, hoping to make a difference in people's lives," Marlene recalls.

The day after graduation, at the age of seventeen, she began working for the *Arizona Republic/Phoenix Gazette* and remained there for fourteen and a half years, moving steadily forward into positions of more and more responsibility. Today, as Community Relations Director for KTVK TV3, the ABC affiliate in Phoenix, she serves as liaison between the station and the community, actively serving on the boards of a variety of organizations. She organizes programs and activities to heighten the station's profile in the community and attends numerous functions as a representative of KTVK.

Marlene, who is single, also teaches a class of college-age students at North Phoenix Baptist Church and still finds time to be a loving daughter to her mother, an encouraging sister to her brothers, and an engaging friend to the rest of us. She is a creative, charmingly verbal, and highly productive person.

When I first met Marlene in the fall of 1984, she interviewed me for a singles' conference held at her church. The plane had arrived late, I had missed connections with my airport contact, and my luggage hadn't arrived with me.

So, there I was at the interview—frazzled, hungry, and dead tired. The last thing in the world I wanted to do was answer a lot of questions—until I started talking to Marlene Klotz. Those kind, soft eyes kept affirming me, and her warm spirit made me completely relax. In no time we were into a fun repartee that we never wanted to end.

After the interview, Marlene took me to dinner, and for the remainder of the weekend I became the contented recipient of her attention and generous hospitality. We've been close friends ever since.

This interview took place the summer of 1986 when Marlene and I took a Caribbean cruise together.

Luci: "You do see the trend here, don't you, Marlene?"

Marlene: "What do you mean?"

Luci: "I mean, you do see how, from your earliest years, you had a sense of community? From trying to teach toddlers how to read when you were five to planning an event related to the Salvation Army or United Way, you're a born community relations director. Always involved. Always organizing. You see that, don't you?"

Marlene: "That makes a lot of sense, Luci, but I never really thought about it, quite frankly. I never thought about what I'd do except maybe be a school teacher. But it's interesting because the characteristics that were being nurtured back then make up who I am today."

Luci: "Were you competitive in school?"

Marlene: "Oh yes, very. Not athletically, but when I took on a project I wanted it to be the very best it could be."

Luci: "But more than competitive, I see you as caring. Every project had to do with people and their needs."

Marlene: (Thinking a few minutes, then looking away nostalgically) "Yes, that comes from my mom, I'm sure. Mom's a very compassionate person, and in her own subtle way, she's been the biggest positive influence in my life. From her . . . by watching her example . . . I learned how to care for people and want to reach out to them."

Luci: "Tell me about your newspaper work. . . . Did you like it?"

Marlene: "Oh yes! When I first started with the paper, I was taking classified ads over the phone. But they knew I liked to write and had some writing skills, so after eight months they transferred me into the promotion department. Then things started happening. You know, I would barely get one thing under my belt and really moving in it, then they'd move me into another area. I was also very involved in an advertising club, a local club for people under thirty. That, combined with the opportunities of the paper, gave me the real outlets to develop my creative abilities."

Luci: "In this community outreach, were you ever discouraged? Did you ever feel you weren't on the right path or wouldn't end up where you wanted to go?"

Marlene: "Not really, because I had no big plans. I was just doing what I liked to do."

Luci: "Moving forward without a lot of thought or planning?"

Marlene: "Yes. That's right. I've been very blessed, and I've recognized that all along. I may not have given God the credit He deserved, because I didn't become a Christian until I was twenty-eight—ten years into my career. One thing just happened after another, as if I was just going down a road toward something.

"If I *was* ever discouraged it wasn't over a feeling of being on the wrong path. It was more like dealing with things outside of my control . . . discrimination from time to time or the 'good ole boy' network you have to deal with. But it's never been anything where I've gone home at night wanting to beat my head against the wall—I don't feel I ever went through sexual harassment or anything like that. No, I've had a great career, and I know it and I'm unspeakably grateful for it. Doors have always opened."

Luci: "Marlene, do you think having a successful career has anything to do with being in the right place at the right time?"

Marlene: "Yes, but I think we make some of our own opportunities, too, because even if you are in the right place at the right time, if you haven't prepared yourself and shown what you're capable of doing, the opportunity doesn't do you any good at all. I've worked with people who have been in the right place at the right time, and they're still back there. They haven't done anything with it."

Luci: "Good point, Mar. . . . Now, tell me what ingredients you think it takes to make a Christian professional woman."

Marlene: "That's hard to answer because there are several qualities I would list at different times. But I think a dedication to one's moral and spiritual standards is right up at the top of the list. That's a real key. The Golden Rule is critical . . . doing unto others. Also, being God-centered, believing in the Lord with a sincere desire to live as He would want us to. And a love and compassion for people, particularly in this day and age. With all the hard people we have out there, I think the world needs soft people, if you know what I mean. People who are willing to stop and care—touch someone's shoulder, touch someone's life in a different way."

Luci: "Do you think it's possible to be a Christian professional woman and not know it?"

Marlene: (After some thought) "Yes, I believe it is,

because there are so many definitions for *professional.* There are probably a lot of women who wouldn't consider themselves professionals but who are professionals in a very real sense. Walking with the Lord would make them Christian professionals without necessarily being an executive or president of a company."

Luci: "In other words, being a professional doesn't mean one must have some high-powered job."

Marlene: "I think the point is centered in how we treat people, not necessarily what kind of a position of power we hold."

Luci: "That's an important distinction, I think. As a Christian professional, did you ever have self-doubts? Ever fear you'd fail or that you didn't have the right stuff?"

Marlene: "I've *always* had self-doubts, Luci. I think you know that—I've called you enough times with questions about whether or not I should pursue something, wondering if I had what it took. Remember those phone calls?"

Luci: "Yeah." (I smiled because Marlene's appearance belies her doubts. She's always so together and unruffled, one would think she was brimming with confidence. But, of course, she's human. I tend to forget that with people who do things so well.)

Marlene: "In major undertakings, I always wonder, going in, if it is something I can do. . . . Yet the other side of that is: the bigger the challenge, the more exciting it is. I like that part, and the way those undertakings have been accomplished has shown me that God has been with me. It's just taking things a day at a time. Instead of looking at the mountain, it's climbing the little hills at first and plowing through the projects or dealing with intimidating personalities one at a time."

Luci: (I didn't say anything. I was sitting there thinking how alike we all are, no matter where we are professionally. It's kind of comforting to know that even people in the media can feel afraid or doubt their own abilities.)

Marlene: "You know, Luci, my job *demands* that I reach

out. I have to get out of myself and that's good—good for me and, I like to think, good for other people. Just by being in my position I'm going to do things that are going to affect other people's lives. What I have to remember is that the media is *so* powerful. I try very hard never to abuse that or take that power for granted."

Luci: "You know, Mar, being in community relations and being a Christian, you have wonderful opportunities to live out the commandments of Christ."

Marlene: "Oh yes, it's a perfect platform."

Luci: "Because when He said to love one another, bear one another's burdens, put others before yourself—all those things—He was talking about being a community relations director, wasn't He?"

Marlene: "Well, He was certainly talking to me, if that's what you mean."

Luci: "How does it feel to have your own special calling?"

Marlene: (Laughing) "But we all have that, really. My job just has a little higher profile, and that does add pressure. I want to live a life that reaches other people because I genuinely love the Lord and love others, not because it's my *job* to reach out. It's a subtle difference, but it's there."

Luci: "You never felt you wandered in search of your career?"

Marlene: "No, not really. It's a funny thing, but my professional niche always seemed to be just around the corner, and the path I was on kind of ran into it. I didn't wander around hunting for it. And I know, *I know,* the Lord had His hand on my career the whole time, even before I accepted Him personally. I can look back now and see it. My mom factors in, certainly my bosses, personal relationships, my jobs, interests—everything. That's why I feel so blessed."

Luci: "It's obvious you're happy where you are, Marlene. You are simply living out a bent that first manifested itself when you were five and teaching those little kids what you had learned. It's the same sense of gathering people together and offering them a better way of life.

"By the way, let me ask you something: What do you think of professional support structures—like networking? Do you think it's important to give and receive encouragement among other professionals?"

Marlene: "Oh, Luci . . . we *have* to know that people care about us as human beings. *I* need that. In high-stress positions it's important to have a support structure behind you, whether it be a parent, a spouse, a friend—whoever. Just someone you can turn to when the going gets rough and they will recognize your need. You know, God's always there to talk to, but that can feel very one way at times when you need someone to look you in the face and respond.

"I enjoy giving encouragement to other people. And I have found, in most instances, that when I encourage people they become more vulnerable to me. I think that's very positive because it says you've touched their lives in a meaningful way. And that's what it's all about—bringing a new dimension to people's lives."

Traveler #2:
RUTH CRONIN-FRUITT
(b. March 2, 1952)

FOR THREE AND A HALF YEARS, Ruth and I worked together as Rights of Way and Claims agents for Mobil Oil Corporation's West Coast Pipelines Department. I had been there four years before she came, and I'll always remember my joy when the supervisor told me Ruth would be filling the vacancy left by an agent who elected to retire.

Ruth is one of the most delightful individuals with whom I have ever worked. Bright. Caring. Dependable. Teachable. Fun. Attractive—I'll run out of descriptive adjectives before I run out of accolades for Ruth Cronin-Fruitt. Whether she is straightening a file drawer that's out of whack or planning a company function for almost two hundred people, she is always "Miss Organization." A lovely lady, and a genuine professional.

When I became manager for the Rights of Way and Claims Department and Ruth reported to me, her talents and abilities became even more endearing. And then when I left Mobil for a position at Insight for Living (after this interview had taken place), she was promoted to manager and is still doing a wonderful job.

As a representative for Mobil, Ruth needs a working knowledge of preparing legal documents, acquiring important franchises and permits, and expressing herself well, both orally and in writing. This she does on a daily basis. As an emissary for the corporate world, she must network with attorneys, mayors and city councils, engineers, port authorities, and environmental officials. And as a negotiator for Mobil's activities on the West Coast, she settles claims, deals with private citizens in financial adjustments, purchases and/or sells property. How she manages to accomplish all this and to keep all parties happy at the same time is the magic of Ruth. Even when she's on the opposing side, everyone loves her!

I've often thought how fortunate Mobil is to have a woman like this moving up their corporate ladder. But, more importantly, I'm fortunate to have her as my valued friend.

Before Ruth became a Rights of Way and Claims agent, she worked in Mobil's Employee Relations office for six years. I asked her how she felt in those early days of being an agent. Did she want to leave Employee Relations?

Ruth: "Oh, I was scared to death. I wanted to advance, and I knew that being a representative for Mobil, an agent, would be a terrific job, but I thought 'What have I done? I've gotten into something I know nothing about. I don't have any engineering background. I don't have any drafting experience. This is crazy!'"

Luci: "You don't like change?"

Ruth: "No, I don't."

Luci: "Why?"

Ruth: "It's the 'unknowing' element. I like security, and although most of the changes in my life have been for the better—really, all of them—initially I resist because at the time of the change I'm usually happy where I am. I think, 'Well, how can it be better?' So I fight it. . . . But I always end up going ahead with it. I just fight it within."

Luci: "So you think change, instead of creating a challenge, kind of rocks the boat?"

Ruth: "Yes."

Luci: "Do you think people grow without change?"

Ruth: "No!" (We both laughed.)

Luci: "Then, when the job proves to be something you can do, are you glad you took the plunge?"

Ruth: "Always. I have problems with self-doubts at the beginning of new projects, and because I find I'm my worst enemy, I have a little saying I keep posted on my bulletin board: 'It is seldom the difficulty that defeats us but the lack of confidence in ourselves.' Many times I get to thinking I can't do something, so I have to sit down and get myself 'in order.' Then, when I try it, I find it's never as bad as I feared.

"Sometimes too, it's a title that frightens me. It carries so much weight and responsibility. I think I automatically have to be some great person, somebody I'm not. It's scary . . . so many visions of awful things that are going to happen but never come to pass. I always wonder ultimately, 'Why do I put myself through that?'"

Luci: "Ruth, what would you say are some of the ingredients that constitute a Christian professional woman?"

Ruth: "I would say the first ingredient would be motivation. You have to want to excel, to do the best job you possibly can. Also, motivation gives you the drive to make it through the difficult times in your job. Together with that, I would put a lot of emphasis on my own moral standards. There are certain things I simply wouldn't do to get ahead. Then, I also value patience and understanding."

Luci: "Elaborate on that a bit—the patience and understanding."

Ruth: "Okay. Take patience, for instance. When the going gets tough, it's easy to say, 'I want out of here' and go someplace else where that problem doesn't exist." (She paused for a minute, looking away as though she was recalling a time she had done that.) "But I think that if you sit down, look at what you have, count your blessings, and realize you need to wait, things will get better. If I had left every time the going got rough, I wouldn't be where I am today—I had to learn patience.

"As for understanding—you have to learn that rewards don't come immediately. The patience teaches you to understand that the payoff was worth the wait. It's as if understanding is the gift of patience, because you ultimately come to realize why you had to go through some things. You grow up."

Luci: "Ruth, do you have any regrets when it comes to your professional journey?"

Ruth: (She thought for a few seconds.) "I would say I do, yes. I regret that I don't have a four-year college degree. Sometimes that makes me feel personally inadequate. I can't say I graduated from UCLA or something like that; I have to say Harbor College, which is a junior college. I regret that I didn't continue my education to four years instead of two."

Luci: "Has that held you back?"

Ruth: "No, not with Mobil, it hasn't. But I still feel a four-year degree is important and I wish I had it."

Luci: "Do you think of your work here as a job, a profession, or a calling?" (This proved to be one of the most interesting questions I asked each of these women.)

Ruth: "I consider it a profession, because in a job you kind of go through the motions. But in Rights of Way and Claims work you have to take a lot of classes in order to get the necessary background—real estate, engineering, law, property management, and so on. You're building toward a professional goal by learning these various disciplines. Whereas, in a job, I think you're just taught to handle certain skills. With a profession you're reaching for more of an educational level that you have to achieve."

Luci: "By 'educational level' you mean knowledge, not necessarily a degree?"

Ruth: "Knowledge, right."

Luci: "Ruthie, tell me something—do you lead more with your heart or your head?"

Ruth: "Well, that depends. I'd have to say both. If I am handling a claim, for example, where I'm dealing with a person who has suffered a lot of loss, I try to put myself in that person's position and see his or her point of view, from my heart. Yet, on the corporate end of it, I have to lead with my head because I have to be able to justify any type of decision I make. I'd put importance on both aspects of your question. I don't think I deal with either one exclusively."

Luci: (I had to laugh because there have been times when Ruth tried to have a heart for someone who ultimately wanted to gyp Mobil, and I've seen her switch right over to a head decision. I reminded her of this.) "You'll go with your heart for a certain period of time, but when that's the end, pal, that's the end!"

Ruth: "This is true." (She smiled.)

Luci: "Did you get every job you ever applied for, Ruth?"

Ruth: "No, and this is kind of funny because now I wonder why I even wanted the only job I was turned down for. But anyway, I applied to be a flight attendant—you know, an airline stewardess—and was turned down. To tell you the truth, I don't know why; I went for one interview and they said, 'Sorry . . . we'll call you,' or whatever, and they never did.

"Now, of course, I'm glad I didn't get that job. I think I was twenty or twenty-one then, and it looked like such a glamorous thing to do—flinging trays around at 30,000 feet."

Luci: "How'd you feel when they didn't call you back? Were you disappointed?"

Ruth: "Oh gosh, I was crushed inside, because I thought, 'This is what I wanted to do in life, and now what am I going to do? Life is over.' At twenty you think so differently: 'Well, this is it, my life is finished. Now I'll just go to the unemployment office and apply for any old job.'"

Luci: "And did you?"

Ruth: "Yes. In fact, that's how I got my beginning job at Mobil—at the unemployment office."

Luci: "All right! And here you are in 'any old job.' So you didn't have some big dream to one day be president of Mobil—the first woman president?"

Ruth: "Are you kidding? I wanted to be an airline stewardess, that was all. Isn't every Rights of Way agent a reject from an airline?"

Luci: "Okay, Ruthie, in all seriousness now, tell me—would you like to be Manager of Rights Of Way and Claims?"

Ruth: "You mean, *your* job?"

Luci: "Yes. Do you have aspirations to be in this position?"

Ruth: (She sat there for a long time looking at me.) "Well, I wouldn't turn it down if I were offered it. It would frighten me because of the tremendous responsibility that goes with it. But I think I could do it."

Luci: "No question about it."

Ruth: "It would be like when I first became an agent, I suppose. I'd just start out one day at a time, taking things as they came along, working toward my goals and those of the department. You've taught me that many things are possible that I never thought were. To dream big and work hard.

"But what are we talking about here? You're not going anywhere. I don't ever want you to retire."

Luci: "Oh, even when I leave here, I won't retire."

Ruth: "I know. You'll write books."

Luci: "No, I've always wanted to be an airline stewardess. Think I'm too old to qualify? . . ."

Traveler #3:
CHAR TAYLOR
(b. June 29, 1956)

WEBSTER DEFINES "aerobic" as "alive and active where free oxygen is present"—and that's how I define Char Taylor. She is a roman candle, a bundle of energy, a bouncing ball of activity.

When I first met Char, she was teaching an aerobics class on the 1984 "Insight for Living" cruise. "Lift it, lift it. . . . you ate it, now lift it" were the first words that fell on my ears from her smiling lips. She caused me more pain that summer than I had known in years as I discovered muscles brought back to life from the dead. But we had such crazy fun in class, early each morning, that I dared not miss a workout lest I regret it the rest of the day.

South Carolina born, Char has all the charm and hospitality we expect of southerners. She never met a stranger, and in no time everyone she gets to know is her friend. A graduate of Furman University in South Carolina, she has a B.S. in medical technology with a minor in physical education. Asked if her schooling aided in actually becoming a fitness director, she responds, "Oh, no question about it. Once I had the training, studying the human body, I was fascinated by it. And that's what fitness is all about— keeping the body up to par. After the first few times of being nervous in teaching aerobics, I wasn't afraid. I never felt like, 'I can't do this,' because I really wanted to and I truly loved it. It made me feel wonderful . . . so energetic and alive."

As the owner and director of her own exercise company, "Exermotion," Char thinks in terms of leg lifts. While I measure my day by coffee breaks and mealtimes, she measures hers by the percentage of body fat burned and the number of miles run. It tires me just to watch her work.

Interestingly enough, however, physical fitness isn't Char's primary motivation for teaching and exercising. Being deeply committed to Jesus Christ and the abundant life He offers, she feels her highest calling is to introduce everyone in her classes to the richest way of life possible— physical, mental, and spiritual. Exermotion simply gives her the platform to do this. She has classes for beginning, intermediate, and advanced levels of fitness—classes that include business people, pregnant women, senior citizens, teenagers, and college kids.

Although daily classes last from forty-five minutes to an hour and a half, the benefits of knowing Char Taylor last a lifetime. Caring about people, giving of her time and all that tireless energy—these are the things that matter most to this Christian professional woman.

Char and her husband, Mike, have a two-and-a-half-year-old son, Cal, who is the joy of their lives and an absolute doll. (I plan to marry him someday if it turns out he likes older women.)

Since this interview was conducted, Char and her family have moved from Dallas to Meridian, Mississippi. If you live in Meridian, you're going to want to sign up for one of Char's classes today. And if you live anywhere else in the country, you'll want to figure a way to get her to your church or your club or your neighborhood. But beware! If you eat it, she'll make you lift it. She's the only person I know who gives me a pain in the neck and I love her for it.

Luci: "Char, how do you motivate someone to exercise?"

Char: "Well, a person has to like what they're doing, of course, or they won't exercise. They won't stick with it."

Luci: "How do you make people like it? That's hard, isn't it?"

Char: "It depends on what their goals are. If their goals are to lose weight and to change the way they look, they need aerobic activity: so I sit down with them and go through all the activities that are aerobic—swimming, biking, jogging, walking, aerobic dance, and so on. I let them pick their favorite and second favorite. From that, we set up a program to cover three days of exercise a week, based on what we call 'a prescription'—frequency, intensity, and duration."

Luci: "Is that how Exermotion started—with people coming to you, knowing you were an aerobics instructor, wanting to better their health?"

Char: "Yes and no. Actually, Mike and I bought the company from another couple. They had already chosen that name, *Exermotion,* and we kept it. The whole goal behind the company was to provide a service. It was founded to provide exercise to Christian music, because we were sick of exercising to loud, secular, rock music.

"We wanted some way to lead our non-Christian friends to Christ. We all loved to exercise together, but we felt that using Christian music would be an outreach to the unbelieving community. We would all be having fun, exercising together, but they'd also be hearing about Christ. So we approached various local churches, recreation centers, banks, and so on, offering our services for the use of the facilities in their buildings. We offered to provide music, mats, and programming if they let us use their workout room."

Luci: "And did you get favorable reactions?"

Char: "Oh yes—it was amazing! We were never turned down anywhere."

Luci: "Even though you, as believers, were sometimes asking this favor of unbelievers?"

Char: "Right. And I think part of the reason for that open door was the music. Even though it had Christian lyrics, it was very upbeat, fun, and easy to exercise by. This was in 1983, when contemporary Christian music was just beginning to pick up. We used a mix of secular and Christian music because our choice of Christian music at the time was much more limited than it is now. In fact, we used 45s and made our own cassette tapes."

Luci: "Hard to believe, since we have so much Christian upbeat music today."

Char: "Oh yes, tons. And, Luci, just to show you how the Lord opened doors, one day a call came from Jim Riley, the recreation director at Highland Park Presbyterian in Dallas, inviting Exermotion to move to their new gymnasium. He offered us a wonderful deal. We paid nothing—no overhead. And he did all the advertising, bought all the equipment we needed—sound system, microphones, mats, weights, whatever—for only 25 percent of the profit. *And* if our goal was ultimately to go to 100 percent Christian music, Jim agreed to pay for our albums."

Luci: "Fantastic."

Char: "We jumped at the chance. We started with five classes and added more and more and more until we now have twenty-eight a week, with eight instructors.

"People often come to the classes who are embarrassed

at being overweight and don't want to go to a fitness center or a public gym—they don't want to put on a leotard, you know. But they will come to a church where they can work out with their friends 'as they are.' They love it."

Luci: "And have you seen people come to know Christ through this ministry?"

Char: "Oh yes. And now we use probably 80 percent Christian music and 20 percent secular."

Luci: "What is this work to you, Char . . . a job, a calling, or just plain fun?"

Char: "I'm so glad you asked that, because I really do feel that this is my niche. To me, it's my calling, and let me tell you why. It's because I feel good about it inside. I love being able to work out and help others at the same time. I love to see them set a goal and reach it and understand how it all works.

"It's a real challenge, always trying to think up new ideas to make it enjoyable, new ways to present something. If you can say a calling is just plain fun, then that's it. It's my calling. It's fun. It's me—my niche!"

Luci: "Isn't it interesting, Char, when you're in your niche, you feel different inside. Something in there feels 'right.' Although it's hard to put into words, you can feel it."

Char: "Exactly."

Luci: "In decision making, Char, would you say you lead with your heart or your head?"

Char: "I would have to say my heart."

Luci: "I knew it! You're a heart person right down the line."

Char: "Well, here's the reason, Luci. The eight girls who work for me—we're all best friends. We see each other outside of exercise. We go to church and Bible studies together. Our children are the same age. Several of us have the same doctor. We all know each other very well. I know what hurts them, what makes them happy. So if there's a decision to be made about them, I really do believe I lead with my heart."

Luci: "If you have to confront one of them on some issue or let one of them go, isn't that awfully hard?"

Char: "Oh, tell me! It's the hardest thing. And it's at that point I think, 'Okay, I have to use my head here, to do this,' because emotionally I just wouldn't do it. I wouldn't want to hurt them."

Luci: "I understand. But, do you think the best-run companies are run by the heart or the head—or both?"

Char: (Unhesitatingly) "I think the heart!"

Luci: "Really?"

Char: "I'm talking about Christian organizations. When a director leads just with her head, I don't believe she's as sensitive as she should be to other persons' hurts or needs. I don't think she can put the other person first.

"I think you *do* have to use your head, but not as much as your heart, because somehow I know in my heart, in my being, when I'm making a wrong decision. And when I do that, I can't live with it. It's like a battle inside. When I make decisions with my head leading, it feels cold—or 'heartless,' I guess. I just don't think I can do that."

Luci: "Can you give me an example?" (The reason I camped on this issue and found it so interesting was that I lead with both head and heart, and each of the other women interviewed did the same. Char was the only one who stuck solely with heart decisions.)

Char: "Yes. After Cal was born, lots of opportunities were offered us to teach classes in other places. These opportunities may have involved interrupting Cal's nap or rushing, pushing, shoving to get him ready to go with me. I had to learn to say no. Were he not there, I would say yes and go do it because I enjoy it so much. I'd run all day long. Whatever the needs, I would try to meet them. My head might want to go teach, but my heart says, 'I have a family.

I have a baby. I have responsibilities at home. I need to say no.'"

Luci: "Char, since you believe you have found your niche, your calling . . . what do you think is your secret to success?"

Char: "Well, I've had to learn this. It wasn't easy and it didn't come first—but now, as I look back, I would say obedience to the Lord. I look at what we have and realize that God has given us this as a package. The doors opened—the invitations, the financing, the available facilities. All that was just handed to us. So, because I see that, I yearn to be obedient to Him in what I do. He brought the company to us, and it's so much more than we ever dreamed, that I want to trust Him more and obey Him.

"Then too, there's the people—in obeying God, I love the people who come to my classes, most of whom I don't even know. Our goal with Exermotion is to love the person we work with, the whole person. We try to minister to their hearts and get their minds off how they look or their negative feelings about themselves. We want them to leave having had a good time and feeling good about themselves. Many of the people have busy schedules, carpooling, non-Christian mates, so for them the class is their spiritual boost for the day. Loving them and seeing them be happy is great."

Luci: "Your secret to success, then, is obeying God and loving people as they are?"

Char: "Yes, that's it. And I should add one more thing. I think part of our success is living every moment full-tilt boogie! It's gotta move!" (She was laughing.) "You know that from the cruises, Luci. Remember what fun that was? All that hooting and yelling to the music?"

Luci: "How can I forget, child? I couldn't walk for weeks. And remember when Chuck wore his moose hat to class and everybody wore such crazy gear? It *was* fun."

Char: "Oh, that's exactly what I mean. You're having such fun, you forget you're overweight . . . you're just there enjoying each other, laughing, entering in . . . really, it's a spiritual high!"

Luci: "Char, do you ever want more than what you have in terms of your profession?"

Char: "No, not really. I'm happy about my scheduling and my family. Every now and then I see a wonderful exercise studio and I think, 'Wouldn't it be neat to have a facility like that for Christians,' but I'm not driven to that. I think when you're in your niche, there's a calm, settled feeling inside. It's a pace that's right for you."

Luci: "Does Mike work with you in this?"

Char: "Oh yes. In fact, you should probably be interviewing him, because he's so qualified—much more than I am. He has an undergraduate degree in physical education with an emphasis in adult fitness and a master's in exercise physiology with a minor in health management."

Luci: "Do the two of you have joint goals?"

Char: "Well, yes. Ideally, we'd love to have our own exercise facility, based on Christian principles but open to everybody. Mike would be the director and I the associate. But we feel if we're obedient where we are and loving people, those doors will open if God wants them to. God has blessed us immeasurably where we are, so we're really very happy."

Luci: "In Exermotion, do you pray together as a staff?"

Char: "Definitely. We have weekly meetings and begin each one with prayer. And if there's a problem bothering someone, we put our meeting on hold so we can spend whatever time we need in prayer. Or we call each other on the phone and request prayer about various things."

Luci: "Do you pray for the people in the classes?"

Char: "Yes, often, and by name. I believe this is why everyone is so close. We are always praying for one another."

Luci: "Char, do you ever feel inadequate?"

Char: (Pensively) "Sometimes I do—when I see people in positions equal to mine, who are better qualified in terms of background and education. When that happens, I have to remind myself that it's all of the Lord, anyway. *Many* of the things that have happened to us are surprises. Mike and I would never have dreamed all this would come to us. It just shows us over and over how creative God is."

Luci: "What do you think professionalism means?"

Char: "I think it means simply making whatever it is you do the best it can be. Let me give you an example. There are lots of exercise instructors out there who are *not* professionals. They don't know the format of a class, how it should be done, how to set up a schedule, how to handle people. They're just there, jumping around. But a professional is more than an instructor; she's a leader. In my opinion, a professional is one who makes her work effective over the long haul, who makes a real difference in people's lives."

Luci: "Can a non-Christian woman be a professional?"

Char: "Yes, I think so."

Luci: "Then, what's the difference between her and the Christian professional?"

Char: "Well, the Lord, obviously. The Christian gives the credit of her success to God. The non-Christian takes the credit herself. The Christian's soul is driven by God, while the unbeliever's soul is driven by something else— self or fame or money or power. For the Christian there's more of a balance. For the non-Christian it's just work, work, work, with no end to it."

Luci: "If you had any advice to give the woman who wants to enter your field, what would it be?"

Char: "Well, let's see. . . . Education is of utmost importance. The body is a delicate thing that needs proper attention from people who know what they're doing. So many people who teach aerobics are 'off the street' with no knowledge of body mechanics. This discredits those of us who are trained, and if something unfortunate happens, it gives the rest of us in the field a bad name. The properly trained person knows what the muscles are and how they function. The heart is a muscle, for example, and the qualified instructor needs to know how to handle a heart attack if that happens."

Luci: "Were that to happen in your class, would you know what to do?"

Char: "Oh, absolutely, and so would all my instructors."

Luci: "Any regrets about your profession?"

Char: "Maybe one. I wish I had started sooner with all this. I am an only child, and both my parents are dead. Maybe if I had known more about the value of exercise and proper eating habits, I could have motivated and encouraged them in a healthier life. They might be alive today. I do regret that."

Luci: "If somebody says to you, 'That can't be done,' how do you react?"

Char: "It's like lighting a fire under me, because somehow I'm going to find a way to do it. I believe there's nothing that can't be done if we trust the Lord for it."

Traveler #4:
PAULINDA KRUG
(b. April 16, 1947)

I COULD WRITE A BOOK about Paulinda Krug; we have known each other twenty years. I know her family, and I feel that she and I have been deeply instrumental in each other's spiritual maturing.

Paulinda has been teaching speech communication for eighteen years and presently is affiliated with one of the finest schools in Texas, Trinity High School, which serves a suburban area between Dallas and Fort Worth. Paulinda is responsible for the debate team, which annually brings home trophies by the truckload, as well as oral interpretation, extemporaneous speaking, oratory, competitive acting, and an English class for non-college-bound students.

Talking with Paulinda is exhilarating, although it can get heated at times when she gets in her debate mode. She makes me want to go out, buy the latest newspaper, and read everything in it.

Asked why she so enjoys teaching speech communication, a course of study she has loved since her own high-school days, Paulinda replies, "I think it's the best format for teaching values to students, challenging them to know what they believe and why they believe it."

Paulinda is a first-class challenger. She makes you take a stand because she makes you think. She wakes up that part of your brain that's asleep or twiddling its thumbs. She challenges me every time we're together, and I'm so glad she's on the academic scene to challenge the young people of today.

A single person of high energy, Paulinda is a jogger, tennis player, avid reader, risk taker, and independent thinker. She lives in Euless, Texas, but thinks nothing of flying to Los Angeles or New York just to go to the theater. (Now, there's a woman with her priorities straight!)

Speeding down the freeway on our way to a meeting, with Paulinda driving and me spilling coffee on my skirt, I thought I might as well get right into it:

Luci: "Well, Paulinda, do you still like teaching speech after all these years—still like challenging kids to think?"

Paulinda: "Oh yes, I don't think I'll ever tire of that."

Luci: "Why not? What's so good about it?"

Paulinda: "I think it goes back to when I was in high school, Luci. Back then no one taught me how to solve problems. No one taught me how to make decisions. And I think, generally, that's neglected with high-school students. They're given materials and go through routines, but they don't know what they believe or why they believe it. I like to help them think through their beliefs, to help them know themselves better by enabling them to analyze their own strengths and weaknesses."

Luci: "Do you ever learn anything from them?"

Paulinda: "Definitely! I keep up with the latest fads and fashions, hair styles, slang words and phrases. I've also learned to play a mean game of poker. They've taught me how to lose gracefully."

Luci: "You ever get discouraged?"

Paulinda: "When I lose at poker?"

Luci: "No, in your career."

Paulinda: "Of course. I remember a time in graduate school when I was very discouraged. You'll remember this too. I had just started classes, and my major professor was an outstanding teacher, but he was seemingly a very callous person. I was excited about taking the class with him, but after a couple or three sessions he seemed to be picking on me, disagreeing with my statements, generally belittling me in front of the class. He didn't seem to be doing this to the other grad students."

Luci: "Oh yes, I remember this."

Paulinda: "Well, anyway, I thought, 'I'm not good enough. I'm not cut out for grad school. I won't make it.' And I came over to your place and sat in your kitchen crying, and you said, 'Paulinda, don't take it personally. He's testing you; he's trying to see if you've got what it takes to make it, if you've got the discipline and the endurance and the perseverance. So don't quit. Stay with it a little longer, and it'll work out.'"

Luci: "Did I say all that? Gosh, not bad advice. I just recall your coming over."

Paulinda: (Smiling) "No, you really helped me. Turns out that prof became my favorite in the grad program. He was a great teacher, and I benefited tremendously from his classes. But that encouragement from you taught me some-thing. It taught me that sometimes we need immediate encouragement, and that can come from friends.

"But discouragement also demands something on a long-lasting basis—praying about it. There's a verse that says that a king's heart is in the hand of the Lord and He turns it whichever way He wants. So I began to pray about this prof, believing that if God could change the heart of a king, He could change the heart of my professor.

"I think when we are discouraged professionally we need both to pray, telling God our times are in His hands and ask Him to help us through it, and to seek the support of friends and people we trust. They're both important."

Luci: "What role do you feel a woman's own vision plays in the pursuit of a profession?"

Paulinda: "It's critical. My strength of conviction that I am to be a teacher, for example, gets me past any obstacles, challenges, barriers, or discouragement. If I am convinced that I'm doing what I'm supposed to be doing in terms of God's will, then I'm not going to be deterred in following my career."

Luci: "What ingredients make a Christian professional woman?"

Paulinda: "If the thrust of that question is 'profes-sional' Christian woman rather than 'Christian' profes-sional woman—and I think it is—then obviously Christian ingredients such as godliness, integrity, honesty, and obe-dience would be givens. All those attributes go with being a Christian woman, whether she's in a career or not. So I want to think past that and emphasize the professional part. I equate a professional woman with one who's in a position of leadership where she can be a motivator and a facilitator. That's why I teach. It's the best format for me to influence people in a positive way. Then, there's the purpose of serving others. A Christian professional isn't in it for herself. So, all together, I'd say a Christian profes-sional woman is a woman with biblical standards who is in a position of leadership and whose purpose is to motivate and serve people."

Luci: "That's a good answer. You enjoy being a professional leader, don't you?"

Paulinda: "Sure. I love it."

Luci: "Because of what it does for you, or because of what it enables you to do for others?" (There was a long pause.) " . . . Hello?"

Paulinda: (Laughing) "I was just thinking. The reason I'm teaching is that it enables me to do terrific things for others. Now obviously, that will bring me a lot of personal satisfaction also. So, it's really both. But I do want to help people actualize their potential. That's why I teach. And I'll go a step further. I think the best teachers are those who gain satisfaction from what they have contributed to their students, not those who are in it just to gain a personal reputation or who are on an ego trip. You have to be unselfish and dedicated to be an outstanding educator. I think the best teachers are those who willingly give of their time, energy, and talents."

Luci: "You don't teach for the subject matter, necessarily, but for what you're giving your students that can benefit them throughout their lives?"

Paulinda: "Yes, and many times I never even see the results. While there is some immediate gratification when there is success in contests or when kids say 'thank you' or when I see them grow throughout the year, for the most part I will never see the greatest benefits of my teaching. That will happen after the students are adults and not connected with me at all."

Luci: "Was there ever a time in life when you wandered, Paulinda? In search of your professional path?"

Paulinda: "That's an interesting question. Especially now that you're catching me at this time of my career. After teaching for eighteen years, for the first time I am thinking about what else I would like to do. While I want to be involved in people's lives, decision making, problem-solving, leadership, I am not convinced I should always remain in the classroom to do that. For instance, I'm in the process of writing a curriculum for a leadership course, and that's very exciting to me. I would like to lecture. I'd like to give leadership seminars. So, even though I have never wandered physically, I'm now getting eager to wander mentally.

"When I went to Trinity to teach, I wasn't seeking that position. It came to me. I had been praying for God to provide an opportunity to coach a really successful speech squad—to have kids who were capable of doing really well on local, state, and national levels. He gave me that at Trinity. I've had six years of success on all those levels, and I'm convinced that's God's answer to prayer. But frankly, that's not enough. Now that I've had that experience, I want something else—something more. I'm approaching a wandering phase in my career."

Luci: "So you think wandering can come long after a career has been established?"

Paulinda: "Yes, I do. It's hard for me to imagine people being stagnant in their careers. Not that it's always necessary to change careers after a while. But I think it's the character of the person that makes a career. And people change. As I have developed and matured as a person, as I've been exposed to things, as I've suffered pain, as I've taken risks—all those things in my personal life have brought a depth to my teaching. So my growth as an individual gives me more to bring into my career, more to bring to my students. Therefore, what I mean by wandering is, I think the human soul wanders and continually questions, 'Is this what I'm supposed to be doing? Is this truly fulfilling? Is there something more?' I think that's part of the growth process."

Luci: "Do you have any regrets in your profession, Paulinda?"

Paulinda: "Hmmmm . . . Yes, my regret is that I didn't know at nineteen or twenty-two, when I first began teaching, what I know now. My regret is that I didn't have the insight, sensitivity, perception, training—the personal and professional experience, that I have now. What I have learned as a person has helped my teaching, because for me it's a total thing. It's my job. It's my profession. Really, it's my calling. It involves all of me. What I am as a person is reflected in my classroom."

Luci: "You have a master's degree. Ever wish you had a Ph.D.?"

Paulinda: "No, not really. I've contemplated that, but I'd have to devote so much time. . . . I don't mind the study. I love studying—it's exhilarating, it's challenging. But frankly, it's too big a sacrifice in terms of personal relationships. For me to get a Ph.D. would mean abandoning time with my family and my friends. I don't want to do that. I've kind of done an about-face in that. My career is not the most important thing to me anymore."

Luci: "I remember when you first started teaching, it was all-important, even at the expense of personal time with people you loved. You've changed, then?"

Paulinda: "Yes. And I'm glad. I've learned that people are more important than a career. I think that when I first began teaching, I used my career as an escape, so I wouldn't have to confront personal situations and make decisions. But that's changed now. I still have to sacrifice some time in relationships to fulfill professional responsibilities, but that's one reason I believe God has something else for me professionally—so I can have more time to devote to those people who have been so loving, unselfish, and understanding with me. I believe God's will for me is to be involved with people, whether that means helping students toward optimum self-actualization in the classroom or caring about and addressing the needs of my family and friends."

Luci: "You've grown, Paulinda, and I'm proud of you! Some people go through life and *never* learn the value of touching people's lives."

Paulinda: "I just finished reading an inspiring book that I feel summarizes my personal feelings about teaching. It's about Christa McAuliffe, the teacher who was selected to be aboard the space shuttle Challenger and who died in the launch. The book is entitled *I Touch the Future.* I greatly admire Christa McAuliffe's dedication to upgrading the reputation of professional educators, and she seems to have been a superb person and teacher. Her philosophy expressed in that book is also my philosophy: 'I touch the future . . . I teach.'"

Traveler #5
CYNTHIA SWINDOLL
(b. April 9, 1937)

"FROM THE TIME I was sixteen years old, I wanted to be in ministry. That was when I seriously dedicated my life to the Lord and felt He wanted me to marry either a minister or a missionary."

That statement by Cynthia Swindoll reflects her earliest awareness of her calling. From that moment, God set in motion the circumstances that have taken her to her professional niche. Through triumphs and traumas, joys and sorrows, peaks and valleys, He has brought her to the place where she so effectively serves today as Executive Vice President of Insight for Living, an international radio broadcast and related ministry that centers around the preaching of her husband, Chuck (who also happens to be my brother).

Cynthia is an amazing woman, the stabilizing and loving force behind Chuck's burgeoning ministry. As a mother and grandmother, she is a person of wisdom and compassion. As a Christian professional she is a pursuer of excellence and a creative entrepreneur. Never hesitating to offer help or encouragement where it's needed, Cynthia finds her greatest satisfaction in serving others. She has a very tender spirit—still water running deep.

During our interview, I learned things about Cynthia that I'd not known before, although we have been sisters-in-law for over thirty years. I appreciated her openness and vulnerability. And I enjoyed hearing firsthand about the beginnings and development of Insight for Living:

Cynthia: "When we started, there were certain things that were very important to Chuck and me—especially the integrity with which we would conduct our business and the way we would handle fundraising. We wanted to establish a very high standard for our employees, to provide a pleasant working environment and state-of-the-art equipment for maximum efficiency. We had a real commitment to excellence in every detail of every single function, and we wanted a ministry in which we were free to operate that way. But our primary objective was to communicate the Scriptures and their application to our daily experiences. I had an intense desire that people would understand God's Word and experience His power. So my basic responsibility is to make sure all these desires and commitments are carried out with balance. Then, my other responsibilities are . . ."

Luci: "Hold it! Wait. Wait a minute. That first batch of stuff is enough. Don't you get *tired?*"

Cynthia: "Not really. This keeps me going, makes me feel *alive*. I love it and always feel challenged. There are never enough hours in the day."

Brother! That's the truth. Cynthia is a go-getter of the first order. She rarely runs out of energy.

She and Chuck live in Fullerton, California with their two younger children, Colleen and Chuck, Jr. Their two older children are married and live with their families in a nearby community. We are all geographically close enough to spend holidays together, building wonderful memories.

Number-one in Christian radio broadcasting with a

sermon format, Insight for Living has a reputation that is well deserved. Beginning with six employees in 1979, it now has a staff of one hundred fifty people. Its products reflect distinction in every sense of the word. Not only are listeners the recipients of Chuck's knowledge, warmth, clarity, practicality, and humor—but they are also offered a visual feast in terms of books, booklets, calendars, study guides—all produced and/or distributed by "Insight."

Luci: "Cynthia, what hands-on part do you play in this?"
Cynthia: "Because of my position, I get to have my fingers in every single job at Insight for Living. In broadcasting, I'm involved not only in the United States, but in Canada and many foreign countries. We are beginning to translate Chuck's sermons into other languages, and I'm terribly excited about this and the opportunity to do some international traveling. Then, of course, running a nonprofit corporation requires developing budgets, policies, procedures, information systems, products, marketing, communications, and fundraising. I love it all!

"One of my most enjoyable responsibilities is reading every one of Chuck's sermons that we're going to broadcast. From those I get all kinds of ideas. Knowing the communication skills he possesses, I take what he has to say and think of ways we can use it more effectively to help people. I'm very interested in how material is presented. The market is flooded with material, but it's not necessarily presented in such a way that causes people to pick it up and read it. I appreciate art, so I want people on my staff who have abilities in design—or individuals who can be invited in to assist us in developing a product that indeed will be read. We want to produce something that won't be discarded."
Luci: "You mean you read every sermon transcript? Isn't that awfully time-consuming?"
Cynthia: "Yes, it is. And part of the problem is that radio is so daily. A broadcast is every single weekday. I cannot postpone it. I can't even take a vacation from it, really. If

I go away, I've got to do everything ahead of time or as soon as I get back, because those broadcast masters have to go out. There's no putting it off."

Luci: "Has this 'dailyness' ever been a problem to you, Cynthia? I know how conscientious you are about organizing your time. But have you ever misjudged a time frame—promised something you couldn't deliver or had difficulty keeping your word?"

Cynthia: "Those are difficult questions. There are times when it will appear I don't keep my word because of the workload. I have to prioritize my time according to broadcast and printing needs, so if I tell someone I will have something done by such and such a time and a horrendous number of other things are going on—not to mention my family responsibilities—I may not have it done in time. That troubles me very, very much. I'm not always good at determining just how much time it will take to do a quality job, with all the other things that need to be done. That's the bugaboo for me. It really is. But overcoming this problem has become a major thrust in my life, and I do feel I'm moving forward. I look forward to its total resolution someday."

Luci: "Would you say that the time factor is your greatest weakness?"

Cynthia: "Yes. But I think there's a reason for that. Several years ago I went through a period of deep depression. Things just were not going well ever, at any time—that was the way I felt. And after I got out of that time of depression, I suddenly thought, 'I've lost all those years!' So I keep trying to put a few more hours into every day, because I want to make up for all the years I think I lost."

Luci: "Well, that's certainly understandable."

Cynthia: "Also, when your schedule is packed back to back and any one task takes a little bit longer than what you've planned, well . . . it doesn't take too many of those to completely destroy a schedule for a day. So that is my weakest point. I plan too much to do and can't get it all done."

Luci: "Does that lead to being a workaholic, Cynthia?"

Cynthia: "It could. I would say I have to fight that. I absolutely love my work. And I do need to be better balanced."

Luci: "Cynthia, how do you feel about Christian, or rather biblical, information that's geared toward the professional? Are professional people as a group being effectively reached for Christ?"

Cynthia: "It's hard at times to document that. I do know a number of organizations that are providing very effective ministries to career people. But I feel this group is probably neglected somewhat within our society—as far as Christian ministry is concerned. This is unfortunate because professionals are consistently on the front edge of so much that is done with excellence in so many areas. What they see every day is quality, so we must reach them on their level with quality services and materials."

Luci: "Do you ever get discouraged or depressed now, Cynthia?"

Cynthia: "Very rarely, but sometimes."

Luci: "How do you handle that?"

Cynthia: "I try to put creative energy into moments of discouragement." (She stopped for a moment and looked at me with very soft eyes.) "I can honestly say that in years past I have experienced a tremendous amount of depression, probably more than the average person will ever have. But now the first thing I do when I get low or depressed is to put energy into whatever is causing the depression. I ask myself, 'What is the right thing to do relative to this issue?' And then I do it. My depression usually does not last more than a half day."

Luci: "What generally makes you low as it relates to Insight? Is it usually money problems—like not having enough funds to operate—or people problems?"

Cynthia: "I think discouragement related to funds is sort of like health problems. I believe God brings those things about, and I have a very quiet confidence that He will solve the problem as long as I'm in obedience to Him in doing whatever we need to do to generate funds.

"So, I guess my greater discouragement comes with people issues. I can think of times when I realized I had been involved in creating a problem. Or, even more painful, there have been times when I realized someone on our staff—someone we loved dearly—was not quite qualified to do the job. I have had to face that and do something about it, and that hurt more than anything I've ever had to do in management!"

Luci: "Do you think it's possible, Cynthia, to transcend some of our problems as Christian professional women by trying to see things from God's point of view?"

Cynthia: "Absolutely! For instance, when I'm discouraged about something at Insight for Living, I remember that God is in sovereign control of our lives. This is an opportunity for Him to reveal His power in this particular situation."

Luci: "And you do honestly think He will?"

Cynthia: "Yes, I do! When those moments happen, I begin to anticipate what God might do to bring a solution. I love to witness God's creativity. Problems really should be challenges to us. They're a launching pad upon which God's miracles occur—or direction is given, decisions made, skills developed. And we can experience in the most full, wonderful way what God has promised us as believers. His power is indeed sufficient. We're the ones who limit it."

Luci: "Have you felt personal growth since you've been involved with Insight for Living?"

Cynthia: "Tremendous growth. I have felt different in every part of my being as a result of doing this. It's been life-changing—it really has!"

Luci: "How do you view your place in the working world? I've asked this of the other women I interviewed, and I want to ask you. Is what you do a job, a profession, or a calling?"

Cynthia: "Basically, I consider it a calling, but I also

consider it a profession. This is probably not what you'd find in a dictionary, but for me, at least, my profession has my heart in it so it's not just a job. I can remember in the past when I pulled weeds in the yard—that was a job! My heart wasn't in it, but it had to be done."

Luci: "Exactly. I have some things that I look at as jobs in my profession. They aren't the part of my work that motivates my heart. A job may pay the rent, but that which motivates me for action, love, and dedication is my calling from the Lord."

Cynthia: "That's right. There may be some areas of my responsibility now that I may think are 'jobs' I wish I didn't have to do, but I can't think of very many. Probably one area would be in addressing negative correspondence. That's very hard because usually the person has misunderstood something because he or she doesn't have the complete perspective on an issue."

Luci: "In your mind, what constitutes professionalism? What are some of the ingredients?"

Cynthia: "Well, first of all, I have to say that I believe because God said it so many times, particularly in the Old Testament, that He wants us to be obedient. 'Obey My Word. Do what I tell you to do, and you will experience success.' So I feel that, number one, we've got to be obedient to God's Word. And sometimes, apart from whatever may be considered right or wrong professionally, there are things that are spiritual rights or wrongs in business. I feel you have to have knowledge. You have to be growing in your knowledge and then obedient to the knowledge you have gained."

Luci: "You mean like walking in the light. The more light you have, the more responsible you are to walk in that light."

Cynthia: "Yes, that's right. Then, second, I feel you need to have an intense love for people, not only for the people you're working with, but the people you're working for—the people you're trying to serve. People who for the most part you will never meet. If you have a love for them, you will want to communicate something to them that will truly make their lives better.

"Something else that I really live by is a quote from Jim Elliot: 'Wherever you are, be all there. Live to the hilt every situation you believe to be the will of God.' We need to live life with all our might, with all of our gusto, with every fiber of strength that we have in our being. That's why there's not anything I do that I don't enjoy. I want to put every kind of energy I possibly can into whatever is a part of my everyday experience."

Luci: "My sentiments exactly! But I want to ask you further: Do you look for these same ingredients in the staff that you hire?"

Cynthia: "Let me put it this way: I find that the professional people I work with who do have these ingredients in their lives really help us in putting together every aspect of our ministry. For example, take the secretary who helps me in answering all my correspondence. I need someone who can address the need of an individual who writes us, communicating a caring concern for him or her as a person. I need someone who can perceive the deeper need that is somehow communicated in their correspondence, although not in actual words. I feel for the most part the people who work for us have that special kind of quality in their lives."

Luci: "That's great. Would that every organization were like that. Now, a few more questions before we quit. . . . What do you like most about being a professional woman?"

Cynthia: "I think it's the everyday interaction and the challenges of all that we have discussed. I like being a vital part of life. And, you know, people can experience that if they want to. I'm amazed at the number of people I hear of who are bored; I think there's way too much out there to do for anybody ever to be bored!"

Luci: "I couldn't agree more. Now let's see, is there anything else? Tell me this: Has your position with Insight—

handling the huge workload and making decisions—made you a better manager in your own home? Has it made you a better mother?"

Cynthia: "Oh, definitely. I believe it's made me better all the way around. As an example, things I used to do for the children, they've now learned to do for themselves. A while back, 100-percent-cotton garments were 'the thing,' and when I went shopping with Chuck, Jr., he chose these 100-percent-cotton shirts and pants. I said to him, 'Chuck, I don't have time to iron all those clothes.' He said quite independently, 'Oh, I'll do my own ironing,' and he's doing it!"

Luci: "One final thing, Cynthia. Do you still have professional dreams or goals?"

Cynthia: "Well, I guess as long as I can see needs, whether in the public or at home, and can create or develop ways and resources to address those needs, I will have dreams and goals. I'm not afraid to tackle anything.

"I guess there are occasions when I wonder what I would do if something happened to Chuck, especially during these years when I have a lot of energy. I certainly feel that Insight for Living could go on. A lot would depend upon our having another excellent speaker and the effectiveness of that person's ministry. But I certainly feel the basic tools we have, the procedures we have developed, the policies, the employees who work at Insight could be tremendously effective in other ministries.

"I don't see myself ever retiring, though I know at some point I may have to face that issue."

Luci: "You don't have the time, for one thing."

Cynthia: "Right, I don't. But I believe if the time comes that a change has to be made, I will go into it with just as much gusto as I have this, and hopefully would experience as great a measure of satisfaction.

"If God opens a door, I'll be the first to march through, eagerly anticipating the demonstration of His miraculous power."

chapter six

The
Niche

It is not what I do that matters, but what a sovereign God chooses to do through me. God doesn't want worldly successes. He wants me. He wants my heart in submission to Him. Life is not just a few years to spend on self-indulgence and career advancement. It's a privilege, a responsibility, a stewardship to be lived according to a much higher calling—God's calling. This alone gives true meaning to life.

—ELIZABETH DOLE
National Prayer Breakfast Address
February 5, 1987

MAGDA OLIVERO invited us to lunch in her Milan apartment. An elevator took us to the second floor, where the door opened and we stepped into another world—a world of antiques, paintings, Persian rugs, rare books, lovely furnishings, and an enormous grand piano that dominated the living room. On every wall and in every hand-carved cabinet were displayed memorabilia from this great singer's years with the opera, including gifts from various nations. She gave us a little tour as we awaited the arrival of her husband, Aldo, who was coming home for lunch.

Everything was quality! The china on which we ate. The crystal from which we drank. The chairs on which we sat. The white-gloved maid who served our table. The recorded music that drifted across the living room. Everything. Even the conversation was quality nourishment for the mind and heart. But that was only the beginning.

After Aldo had returned to his office, the driver of the car Magda had hired picked us up in front and took us to Lake Como for the afternoon. This beautiful lake is about twenty-five miles north of Milan. Magda especially wanted us to see the famous Villa d'Este, built in 1550, that was situated beside the lake. She would be our guide since she had been there many times and knew the area well.

There were four of us—Magda, the driver, my friend Charlotte, and myself. We chatted about many things along the way, in English and Italian, seeking to make ourselves understood with appropriate sign language. (It helps immeasurably in Italian/English conversation if one is accustomed to talking with one's hands.)

Occasionally, I have to admit, I went off on my own

musings: *Pinch yourself, Luci. Are you really here? With Magda Olivero, the Magda Olivero? Savor this moment, kid. You're on top of the world.*

When we arrived at the lake, I was indeed on top of the world. Lake Como lies at an altitude of six hundred fifty feet, in a depression surrounded by mountains reaching from two thousand to eight thousand feet—snowcapped and stunningly beautiful. The day was clear, with a chill of leftover winter wind in the early April air. The first blush of spring had settled onto branches of oleander, chestnut, fig, and pomegranate trees that lined the luxuriant lakeshore.

Hotel officials greeted Magda warmly when we walked in. They knew her well and escorted us to a table near the window overlooking the lake, while our driver waited for us in the car. He would have an hour's wait.

We ordered tea. My mind left the scene again: *This is unbelievable. How can this famous woman, with all she has to do, take this kind of time to leisurely show us Lake Como? Give up an afternoon. Treat us like royalty. What kind of woman is this?*

Magda told us the lake is famous for its natural beauty. Sportsmen flock there annually to fish for trout, eel, and herring. A private club for boating and swimming is available. Standing on the shore, one can look to the north and see the Swiss Alps, although we were in Italy.

Magda loved this place, you could tell. She liked to recall fond memories of earlier visits. And the people at the hotel obviously loved her; she was treated like a great lady.

It's no wonder. Magda had enjoyed a remarkable opera career in Europe. Her sensitive interpretations of various opera roles had made her famous worldwide. At the time, Charlotte and I had only known her a year; we had been working with The Dallas Opera Company when Magda made her American debut there in 1967. But in her presence that day, we felt like two of the most important people in her life. We didn't realize until later, as we had opportunity to know her better, that Magda had the rare ability of making everyone feel this way. Stories had been told of how famous aging composers had either written specific works or resurrected earlier compositions just for her vocal and dramatic gifts. In turn, she responded to them that she would do the part as the *umile ancella* (humble servant) of the composer.

And here we were, the two of us, the guests of Magda Olivero in this breathtakingly gorgeous spot. That day, that place, that feeling are etched in my memory forever.

Two years later, while vacationing in Europe, I visited Magda at her summer home in Rapallo, Italy. Rapallo is a small, picturesque village immediately to the northeast of Portofino, on the Ligurian seacoast—a heart-stirring region in all its beauty. It is that upper portion of the Italian boot that seems to be spilling over in small treasure-towns—like toys out of a Christmas stocking. Every turn of the winding road has an unexpected surprise of lush foliage and color: funny, charming little houses lined with clay pots of fragrant flowers, zigzagging trails, vistas of jagged rock formations juxtaposed against nooks and crannies of luxuriant vines, freshly painted terraces of restored villas, and ever the boat-filled harbor with bobbing yachts and skiffs. There are a million delights to the eye. One cannot absorb them all.

I was sitting one afternoon with Magda at the picture window that overlooked this abundance of visual delight. I was again overcome by it all—the view, the beauty of the day, Magda's person and reputation, the fact that I was actually sitting there in her presence, all that she had, all that she meant to so many people. In a moment, almost without thinking what I was saying, out of the depth of my soul sprung, "Magda, how does it feel to be you?"

She looked at me rather quizzically. I'm sure she was caught off guard by such a forthright question. "What do you mean?" she asked.

"Well, how can I say it . . ." I thought for a minute, looking out the window trying to gather up every Italian word I had ever learned. Using sign language to enhance my efforts, I continued, "Look at you. You have every-thing—two gorgeous homes, lovely furnishings, an envi-able career, fame, money, a husband who adores you, audiences who laud you and fall at your feet, power—everything. It's fantastic. How does it feel to be such a successful woman?"

She was looking at me all the while, smiling, trying to comprehend what I was saying, as I ticked off the things I so admired and envied. She had a very sweet expression on her face and in her eyes. When I finally stopped and let her get a word in, she gave me one of the richest, most treasured gifts I've ever received. It was a message that altered my thinking from that moment on.

Slowly, she began, "Luci, this isn't success"—she ges-tured—"all these things. It's nice to have them, don't mis-understand me. I love things, and it's gratifying to know I can live comfortably, surrounded by beauty."

She paused, trying to decide how to continue. "It's nice not to have material needs, but I don't call this success. To me, success is giving myself to my public. It is knowing that I have touched people with my talent—my singing and acting—my life. It's the effect I have on the people who come to hear me, the people I have made richer because they heard me. That's success.

"When I was young, I used to think success was having all these things, but it's not. Once I found that out, I was a new person. I then had something really important.

"You know, Luci, when I die I want to die on stage—giving myself, my all, to my public. That's the greatest ful-fillment there is, to think that what I have inside can make a difference to somebody else. That's what life is all about."

I just sat there. What a response, from such a "great depth of being," as Emerson calls it. I loved—*loved*—that answer. I began to view success and professionalism differ-ently from that moment on. Magda was right and for the first time I knew it. Something clicked in my head.

There is a world of people out there who are operating under the assumption that they have finally reached their professional niche because they have a title, have accumulated a great deal of money, are able to wield a lot of power, are surrounded by a hefty number of expensive trappings, control a large group of people, burn the midnight oil at the office, and/or cause others to be intimidated by their presence. They have built for themselves an empire. But what about the people outside their castle? What about people they have to be in contact with every day?

Contrary to some opinions, life doesn't begin and end in ourselves. Sometimes we think that people don't know when we shortchange them in our treatment of them, or that they are unaware of our lack of integrity when we cheat them out of giving them our very best.

Read the words of newscaster Linda Ellerbee, who deals with these issues every day in the world of television:

> It's up to those of us who work in the business to be honest reporters—and to learn our craft to make sure that we know how to write, that we produce television and not radio, and that we leave a little something for our audience to do. . . .

Ms. Ellerbee is not suggesting that the people to whom we give ourselves have no responsibility to make wise use of the information that is passed on to them. On the contrary, she's trying to show that when we give our best, others will know it and they too will respond with their best. Integrity breeds integrity. She goes on:

> We at our end have to put in the best we have to offer, because at the other end is a viewer who deserves the best—and knows the difference. That viewer is our audience, even if it's an audience of one, which it's not.[1]

Cynthia Swindoll, in her own way, said these same things in her interview. So did Marlene Klotz, who, like Ellerbee,

is in television. It is our obligation as Christian professionals to give our best to others, adding dimensions to their
lives, so that others, in turn, will want to give their best.
And don't kid yourself, your public—those you encounter
in your professional life—knows when it's getting the best
from you. They can tell the fresh from the leftovers.

Occasionally I am asked the question, "How does it feel
to be in your professional niche?" The inquirer is not asking, "What are the steps in getting there?" or "How long
does it take to arrive?" Those are other questions, entirely
different in nature. When someone asks how it "feels," she
is asking for an emotional response from my heart, not an
objective one from my head. It's like my asking Magda,
"How does it *feel* to be you?"

That's not an easy question to answer, because whenever
we try to define emotions, words seem inadequate. They
are tools of the mind, not the heart. But I have thought
about that question for years and have finally come up with
an answer, although I'm forced to use words to tell you
since language is our medium of information exchange.

I trust this down-to-earth example will capture how it
feels to be in my professional niche: It feels like being a hot
apple muffin.

I'll explain.

One of my favorite foods on this earth is fresh, hot,
homemade apple muffins. I make them occasionally on
Saturday mornings when I have time and can enjoy them in
a leisurely way with freshly ground coffee. I take the
muffin, the cup of coffee, the newspaper, and sit on my
front porch with the neighborhood cats, relishing the beginning of a new day with all of my senses pleased. It's the
next thing to heaven. . . . (See what those muffins do to
my thoughts. I'm digressing.)

When you bake apple muffins, you put all the ingredients together: flour, butter, baking powder, eggs, milk,
apples, a pinch of cinnamon, vanilla. All these go into a
bowl and are blended together. But this blending does not
make the muffins; it only makes the mixture, the goop. So,

you spoon the goop into muffin tins and then put the tins into the oven.

Here's where the transformation takes place. The heat from the oven changes the mixture into edible food. When they're done, the finished muffins don't look like the original ingredients in the mixing bowl. Ingredients in a bowl have no life. They are changed by the addition of energy (heat). Both the mixture and the heat are essential for the outcome of hot apple muffins.

When the procedure is over, the muffins are food for the hungry. And when a muffin enters a mouth, it satisfies. The muffin is satisfied because it's fulfilling the function for which it was made, and the eater is satisfied because hunger is relieved.

My professional life is a mixture. It has a great deal of hard work in it, taking hours of time, concentration, discipline, and sacrifice. To be a professional involves risk-taking and numerous transitions. It demands that I use my head *and* my heart. It has the need for delegation, relegation, deferment, courage, humor, a pinch of craziness. All those things and more.

But without energy, this mixture is just so much lifeless goop. It's not "edible," if you will. The hungry recipient who comes into contact with my mixture of traits will not be satisfied until I give them my blend, hot out of the oven. I need to be energized by the Holy Spirit to satisfy successfully the hunger of those with whom I come in contact.

We can give ourselves to the people around us in a meaningful, eternal, fulfilling way when we permit ourselves to be transformed by God's energy. We've got to stay hot, tasty, and fresh if we're to be food for the hungry.

Recently I went with a group of friends to see and hear talk-show host Oprah Winfrey. You talk about a hot apple muffin—wow! Everybody wanted to eat her up. Full of energy, humor, and warmth, she was thoroughly captivating to a sold-out house. For an hour, she told us about her life, her thoughts, and some of the difficulties she's come through in her rise to stardom. She did several dramatic readings and brought the house down.

I can't remember when I was so deeply moved or entertained. Oprah discussed her faith, her trust in God, her dependence upon the Scriptures, her professional aspirations. Nobody in the audience wanted the evening to end.

But about thirty minutes before the close of her program, Oprah opened it up to receive questions from the floor. Hands shot up everywhere. Men, women, blacks, whites, young people, older people—everyone wanted to ask something.

One question was, "To what do you attribute your success?" She said, "I think it is the fact that I try to treat people the way I want to be treated. That's what makes anybody successful. Every one of you out there can be great if you treat people with love and respect and understanding. You may not be *famous*, but you can be great." As she was talking, I thought about Luke 9:48, which clearly teaches that our care for others is the measure of our greatness.

Oprah went on to say that if you have confidence in yourself, mixed with faith in God, there's no limit to what you can do. I cheered. My sentiments exactly! Oprah gave herself to her public, and we just ate her up.

For those of us who are Christian working women, there are some wonderful verses in Matthew 20 that should be our guide for leadership. Jesus says,

> Among the heathen, kings are tyrants and each minor official lords it over those beneath him. But among you it is quite different. Anyone wanting to be a leader among you must be your servant. And if you want to be right at the top, you must serve like a slave. Your attitude must be like my own, for I, the Son of Man, did not come to be served, but to serve, and to give my life as a ransom for many. (Matt. 20:25–28, LB)

Boy! Just compare that with the information being printed today on how to rise to the top of your professional ladder. It's not only different; it's antithetical! No two concepts could be more opposite. Jesus calls us to committed servanthood, while the world calls us to constant striving.

We often balk at servanthood. The idea of serving "like a slave" conjures up in our mind a most distasteful image. Rare is the person who wants to know, What can I *give*? Most of us want to know, What can I *get*?

But let me remind us again—each one of us, myself included—that the backbone of true professionalism is character, not empire. Therein lies the key to embracing servanthood gladly.

True professionalism, as you have seen from this book and can perhaps testify from your own life, is contrary to the steps that the world orders. It's not by might or power, but by tranquility mixed with grace. It's not by intimidation, but by courage mixed with vulnerability. It's not by workaholism, but by constancy mixed with balance. And it's not by a system of hierarchy, but by democracy mixed with servanthood. In *every* case it is contrary to the world. But it works.

An article in a recent issue of *Working Woman* magazine told of a twenty-nine-year-old man who was dying of AIDS, and of how his office force rallied round him from the moment they suspected the nature of his illness until the day he died. "Where 'Boss' Stops and 'Friend' Begins" was a loving account of triumph in the midst of tragedy.[2]

As a copy editor for a national magazine, Paul was vague about symptoms that forced him to have a series of medical tests. He referred to the doctor's diagnosis as "stomach problems." However, as his condition worsened, his co-workers became like family to him. Recognizing fear in his eyes and his altered behavior, Paul's fellow employees, instead of backing off, demonstrated constant concern and care. He was reassured of his position as a valued member of the team when he was afraid of being fired because of missing so much work. When Mike, the managing editor, had to assume some of Paul's duties, he was careful not to hurt Paul's feelings. Mike told Paul he "had a few extra minutes to kill and would welcome the work." Paul's supervisor took him to lunch at his favorite restaurant, knowing the bright Christmas decorations would lift his spirits. She also wanted to give him a "pep talk," to tell him he was doing excellent work in spite of his difficult circumstances.

Later, Paul told his friends he had cancer of the stomach. When his chemotherapy treatments left him nauseated and dizzy, he had a hard time getting to work by 9:00 A.M. He was told not to worry about it. Paul would find simple gifts awaiting his arrival—flowers, notes, homemade meals. One person offered to help him with his weekly grocery shopping. Another, trying to boost Paul's morale, brought bagels and orange juice to the office on beautiful days, saying she thought everyone should celebrate.

Paul's illness progressed, and he was admitted to a nearby hospital for treatment. The office staff visited him regularly, focusing their attention solely on Paul, trying to be sensitive to his feelings and his need to know everything that happened in the office during his absence. Because he felt guilty about missing so much work, the staff bagged up poetry that readers had submitted, and took the bags to Paul, telling him he was desperately needed to read the poems and comment on them. And Paul was delighted to have something to do—to feel needed.[3]

During this period Paul's office friends became a sounding board for his anger concerning his disease—anger directed at anyone who happened to visit. As Paul deteriorated physically, his friends were experiencing emotional deterioration. Everyone was on edge. Tempers flared. Each person was trying to deal with bottled-up emotions toward a dying co-worker. But they continued to stand by him.

Ultimately Paul had to be replaced. With only two years of service, Paul was offered a fully paid leave of absence. After months of hospital stays, he finally admitted to his boss the truth about his illness. He had known for over a year that he had AIDS. The editor confessed that from the beginning she had known this down deep in her heart. The love and caring at this point intensified. Fellow employees visited Paul as often as they could. When they weren't able to go (because of colds or flu), they made elaborate cards or sent baskets of goodies to Paul's hospital room. There were days that Paul's anger and fear overwhelmed him, making him cutting and bitter. When friends would call, he would hang up on them. But *never* did Paul's former co-workers reject him or stop visiting him. He was repeatedly assured that he was loved, cared for, remembered. In every possible way, they tried to get across, "We'll be there for you."

His friends read poetry to him, prayed for him, even agreed to assume responsibility for his body after death, when his parents could not be reached. During the last few hours of his life his fellow workers, his "family" by now, kept a candlelight vigil at his bedside. In the early hours of New Year's Eve day, Paul died, the victim of a horrible disease but the recipient of unconditional love and affection.[4]

That is character lived out in the workplace. It is possible for any of us to achieve, once we realize our proper response to people's needs. As Christian women in the professional world, it is our duty—dare I say our *mission* in life?—to be there for people. It is our highest calling. It is the most important part of our professional niche. It is the hope for this world.

When Corazon Aquino, the fifty-three-year-old leader of fifty-five million people, was elected President in the Republic of the Philippines, she brought a new hope and a new courage to that nation. "I am not embarrassed to tell you that I believe in miracles," she declared frankly. "God has a plan for all of us, and it is for each of us to find out what that plan is. I can tell you that I never thought the plan was for me to be President. But it seems it is—it has been necessary to have a woman in this position. Women are less liable to resort to violence than men, and at this time in my country's history, what is really needed is a man or woman of peace."[5]

The Christian professional woman is a woman of peace. She is a woman who believes in miracles. From her first days of wandering to the arrival at her professional niche, she is one who pursues excellence. She may fall, she may be sidetracked, she may even be blocked in for a time, but she never gives up. With heart, courage, brains, and faith, she continually progresses, recognizing that her abilities and strengths come from God. And when her deepest joy becomes giving herself to those around her, she will have truly found her place of greatest contribution.

Suggested Readings

Bolles, Richard. *The Three Boxes of Life*. Berkeley, CA: Ten Speed Press, 1981.

Bridges, William. *Transitions: Making Sense of Life's Changes*. Reading, MA: Addison-Wesley Publishing Co., 1980.

Cousins, Norman. *Human Options*. New York: W. W. Norton & Co., 1981.

Ellerbee, Linda. *"And So It Goes."* New York: G. P. Putnam's Sons, 1986.

Friedman, Sonya. *Smart Cookies Don't Crumble*. New York: G. P. Putnam's Sons, 1985.

Harrison, Patricia, ed. *America's New Women Entrepreneurs*. New York: Acropolis Books, 1986.

Harvey, Joan C., with Cynthia Katz. *If I'm So Successful, Why Do I Feel Like a Fake?* New York: St. Martin's Press, 1985.

Hennig, Margaret, and Anne Jardin. *The Managerial Woman*. New York: Anchor Press/Doubleday & Co., 1966.

Hesse, Hermann. *Wandering: Notes and Sketches*. New York: Farrar, Straus & Giroux, 1972.

Howard, J. Grant. *Balancing Life's Demands*. Portland, OR: Multnomah Press, 1983.

Kufrin, Joan. *Uncommon Women*. Piscataway, NJ: New Century Publishers, 1981.

LaBier, Douglas. *Modern Madness: The Emotional Fallout of Success*. New York: Addison-Wesley Publishing Co., 1986.

Loden, Marilyn. *Feminine Leadership*. New York: Times Books, div. of The New York Times Co., 1985.

McDonald, Gordon. *Ordering Your Private World*. Nashville, TN: Oliver Nelson, div. of Thomas Nelson Publishers, 1984.

McGinnis, Alan Loy. *Bringing Out the Best in People*. Minneapolis, MN: Augsburg Publishing House, 1985.

Meberg, Marilyn. *Choosing the Amusing*. Portland, OR: Multnomah Press, 1986.

Suggested Readings

Naisbitt, John. *Megatrends.* New York: Warner Books, 1982.

Naisbitt, John, and Patricia Aburdene. *Re-Inventing the Corporation.* New York: Warner Books, 1985.

Ogilvie, Lloyd J. *If God Cares, Why Do I Still Have Problems?* Waco, TX: Word Books, 1985.

Peck, M. Scott. *The Road Less Traveled.* New York: Touchstone Books/Simon & Schuster, 1978.

Pentecost, Dwight. *Man's Problems—God's Answers.* Chicago, IL: Moody Press, 1971.

Peters, Thomas J., and Robert H. Waterman, Jr. *In Search of Excellence.* New York: Warner Books, 1982.

Sanders, J. Oswald. *Spiritual Leadership.* Chicago, IL: Moody Press, 1967.

Schuller, Robert. *The Be-Happy Attitudes.* Waco, TX: Word Books, 1985.

Sheehy, Gail. *Pathfinders.* New York: William Morrow and Co., 1981.

Smith, Fred. *You and Your Network.* Waco, TX: Word Books, 1984.

Swindoll, Charles R. *Improving Your Serve.* Waco, TX: Word Books, 1981.

Swindoll, Charles R. *Living on the Ragged Edge.* Waco, TX: Word Books, 1985.

Swindoll, Charles R. *Living above the Level of Mediocrity.* Waco, TX: Word Books, 1987.

Swindoll, Charles R. *Quest for Character.* Portland, OR: Multnomah Press, 1987.

Taylor, Daniel. *The Myth of Certainty.* Waco, TX: Jarrell Books/Word Books, 1986.

Tozer, A. W. *The Knowledge of the Holy.* New York: Harper & Brothers, 1961.

Warschaw, Tessa Albert. *Winning by Negotiation.* New York: McGraw-Hill Book Company, 1980.

Wheichel, Mary. *The Christian Working Woman.* Old Tappan, NJ: Fleming H. Revell Co., 1986.

Ziglar, Zig. *Secrets of Closing the Sale.* Old Tappan, NJ: Fleming H. Revell Co., 1984.

Acknowledgments

DEBTS OF GRATITUDE, which are always a pleasure to pay, go to four women whose expertise added immeasurably to the finalizing of this book.

First, I must acknowledge the indispensable assistance of my friend and typist, Nancy King. She brought to this manuscript order, cohesiveness, and most importantly, legibility. Out of hen-scratching and hurried notes, she corrected grammar, spelling, punctuation, and structure, to make me look good. You're the best, Toots.

Second, what would I do without Marilyn Meberg? My dearest friend, gifted with listening ear and perceptive insight, Marilyn knows what I want to say even before I say it. (Why didn't *you* write this book, Marilyn?) In the midst of a full speaking schedule, a move from one city to another, and the completion of a master's program in psychology, she always had time to hear my ideas and chapters with a loving heart. I bounced many a confused thought off her clarifying mind. Besides . . . she made me laugh when things seemed impossible.

Third, I want to thank Anne Christian Buchanan of Word Books, who was the editor for this book. Anne spent late nights and early mornings to bring closure to this project, and her changes and additions gave clarity where it was needed. She helped me stay on target with her insight and sensitivities.

And fourth, I must express my sincere appreciation to Dale Hanson Bourke, who consented to write the Foreword. As senior editor of *Today's Christian Woman* and president of Publishing Directions, Inc., Dale has to be one of the busiest Christian professional women in America, yet she took time to aid me in this project.

Each of you was there when I needed you most. For this, as well as your friendship, please accept my deepest thanks.

Notes

Chapter 1:   The Wandering

   1. Paul Ciotti, "A Walk in the Woods," *Los Angeles Times Magazine,* Dec. 22, 1985, pp. 23, 24, 36, 38.

   2. Jane Arnold, "The Columnists," *Savvy,* Oct. 1985, pp. 36–40.

   3. Jacqueline Giambanco, "Designing A Corporate Image," *Working Woman,* July 1985, pp. 80–82.

Chapter 2:   The Route

   1. Beverly Sills, *Bubbles* (New York: Bobbs-Merrill Co., 1976), p. 209.

   2. Sills, *Bubbles,* p. 114.

   3. Sills, *Bubbles,* p. 224.

   4. Kaylan Pickford, *Always a Woman* (New York: Bantam Books, 1982), no page number.

   5. Pickford, *Always a Woman,* no page number.

   6. Pickford, *Always a Woman,* no page number.

   7. E. F. Wells, *Successful Supervisor* (Chicago: Dartnell Corp., 1985).

   8. William Arthur Ward, "I Will Do More," *Successful Supervisor,* (Chicago: Dartnell, 1986). Used by permission of the author.

   9. Samuel Chotzinoff, *A Little Night Music* (New York: Harper & Row Pubs., 1964), pp. 89, 90.

   10. Sophia Loren, *Women & Beauty* (New York: William Morrow and Co., 1984), pp. 189–91.

   11. "The Beautiful Dream," *Successful Supervisor* (Chicago: Dartnell Corp., 1986).

Chapter 3:   The Signposts

   1. Charles R. Swindoll, *Three Steps Forward, Two Steps Back* (Nashville: Thomas Nelson Publishers, 1980), pp. 17, 18.

   2. Mary C. Crowley, in *America's New Women Entrepreneurs,* ed. Patricia Harrison (Washington, D.C.: Acropolis Books, 1986), p. 79.

   3. Linda Swindall, "Delegate, Delegate!" *Working Woman,* July 1985, p. 23.

   4. Douglas LaBier, *Modern Madness: The Emotional Fallout of Success* (Reading, Mass.: Addison-Wesley Publishing Co., 1986), p. 76.

159

5. LaBier, *Modern Madness,* p. 77.

6. Heather Evans, "The Plight of the 'Corporate Nun,'" *Working Woman,* Nov. 1984, p. 63.

7. Gail Sheehy, *Passages* (New York: Bantam Books, 1984), p. 513.

8. Joan Kufrin, *Uncommon Women* (Piscataway, N.J.: New Century Publishers, 1981), p. 30.

Chapter 4: The Roadblocks

1. Pauline Clance, quoted in Elizabeth Christian, "'Fakes' Scared of Being Found Out," *The Los Angeles Times,* Dec. 8, 1985, sec. 6, p. 24.

2. Dale Hanson Bourke, "Danuta Soderman: Can We Talk?" *Today's Christian Woman,* Jan./Feb. 1987, p. 34.

3. Daniel Taylor, *The Myth of Certainty* (Waco, Texas: Word Books, 1986), p. 113.

4. Taylor, *The Myth of Certainty,* pp. 123, 124.

5. Gail Sheehy, *Pathfinders* (New York: William Morrow and Co., 1981), p. 445.

6. Jane Ciabattari, "The Biggest Mistake Top Managers Make," *Working Woman,* Oct. 1986, p. 55.

7. Donna Kordela, "Small Talk: Chitchat That Leads to Serious Discussion," *The Executive Female,* Dec. 1985, p. 33.

8. Marilyn Meberg, *Choosing the Amusing* (Portland: Multnomah Press, 1986), p. 58.

9. Meberg, *Choosing the Amusing,* p. 59.

10. Meberg, *Choosing the Amusing,* pp. 71–73.

11. Marilyn Loden, "Managing the Woman's Way," *Newsweek,* Mar. 17, 1986, p. 46.

Chapter 6: The Niche

1. Linda Ellerbee, *"And So It Goes": Adventures in Television* (New York: G. P. Putnam's Sons, 1986), p. 250.

2. Leah Booth, "Where 'Boss' Stops and 'Friend' Begins," *Working Woman,* Feb. 1987, pp. 70–74, 110.

3. Booth, "Where 'Boss' Stops," p. 74.

4. Booth, "Where 'Boss' Stops," p. 110.

5. Pico Iyer, "Cory—Woman of the Year," *Time,* Jan. 5, 1987, pp. 18–33.